At the CROSSROADS of Life

WHERE ARE YOU GOD?

TED RICCI

XULON PRESS

Xulon Press
2301 Lucien Way #415
Maitland, FL 32751
407.339.4217
www.xulonpress.com

Unless otherwise indicated, Scripture quotations taken from the King James Version (KJV) –*public domain.*

Printed in the United States of America

ISBN: 978-1-6269-7087-8

DEDICATION PAGE

W ith my love and a heart filled with praise and thanksgiving, I dedicate this book to my Lord and Savior, Jesus Christ. He has transformed my life by His love, His mercy and His amazing grace. He has truly blessed my life with His goodness and His guidance, especially in the darkest days, in the valley of the shadow of death.

In memory of my precious wife Gayla: I thank the Lord for bringing her into my life. I'm was blessed that she was a godly woman of compassion, strength, wisdom and prayer. She was a blessing to our family, a gift from God and is greatly missed!

To my family: My son Jason, his wife Rachel and and my grandkids, Evelyn and Torin; to my son Sean and his wife Amanda, and to my son Justin, thank you for bugging me about writing this book. I love you all and I am blessed to be your Dad.

To three godly teachers that impacted my life while I attended Bible College: Charles Shafer, Jim and Lois Schaefer, thank you for being the servants of God that you are.

TABLE OF CONTENTS

Chapter One

LOOKING BACK

Let's begin our journey as we look back and I share with you some of my past history. I was born in White Plains, New York and spent most of my early childhood years in the Silver Lake section. My dad, Ted (who I was named after) was a master carpenter. My mother, Rose, worked in a doughnut shop as a waitress. As the years went on, trouble came to our home. I would witness my dad and my mom arguing a lot. Dad would get physically abusive with her, especially when he would find the liquor bottles she would hide around the house. The trouble was my mother had a drinking problem. Some call this problem a disease. Funny thing is this disease can be purchased in a bottle or in a can. Alcoholism is an addiction as well as a sin. My mom also tried to commit suicide several times by overdosing on sleeping pills.

I never knew until the last week of her life why she was so troubled and so depressed. I remember one night when I was about eight years old waking up my dad and asking him for a glass of water. He told me to go ask my mother. When I tried to wake her up she would not respond. My dad finally got up and after he put on the bedroom light he saw the empty pill bottle by her nightstand. She was trying to end her life again. The rescue squad came and transported her to the hospital.

1

After they pumped out her stomach, she was stabilized. She recovered after a short hospital stay and soon returned home. Things never did get any better after that day.

This all happened when we lived on 12 East Park Avenue. Our family shared a two family house with my grandmother Mary, my mother's mother. Her first husband, Rocco was a rough character. My cousin John visited our grandfather's hometown in Italy one year. He was asking a lady that he met in the area about where he could find where his grandfather lived. When this lady heard my grandfather's name mentioned, John said she was terrified and she didn't even stick around long enough for him to find anything out. During prohibition times he had ties with organized crime and was transporting alcohol from Connecticut to New York. On one occasion my grandmother hired a private investigator to see if he was having an affair with another woman. He was a real ladies' man or so it seemed.

One day my grandfather told her that he was going away on a business trip. He told her he would be away for about a week. She found out he was going on a cruise and where the ship was docked. On the day he was to leave she came down to pay him a surprise visit. As she spotted him just before he was to board the ship she noticed another woman running up to him and calling his name. This woman gave him a very long embrace and as my grandmother approached them she over heard the lady say something about the trip to him. When he spotted my grandmother his trip turned into a nightmare. My grandmother soon checked to see his registration on the ship and found him listed as Mr. and Mrs. Rocco DiPietro. That was all she needed to see along with the little episode she had already witnessed.

She told him not to come back home and that she was filing for divorce. They were soon divorced after that cruise incident. Several years later she remarried another Italian man by the name of Serge.

Hospital visits after hospital visits. Doctors after doctors, nothing or no one seemed to help my mom. Finally my dad had enough and moved me and my two sisters, Cecelia and Mary, out of the house. We moved to Sleepy Hollow (North Tarrytown) New York to live with my grandfather and my grandmother, Dominick and Cecilia Ricci. The year was 1967 and I was eleven years old. My dad took a trip to Mexico to somehow get a divorce. He came back home to serve the papers to my mom and told her he would arrange visitation with us. All she had to do is agree and sign the papers. What she said to him was extremely shocking and hurtful when I found out. She said "give me $100.00 and I'll sign the papers for the kids." Her state of mind was very disturbed I guess. I always wondered why she would not fight for her kids. It wasn't until several years later that I did end up visiting with her. I will share that incredible time with you later.

In the book of Job 14:1, "Man that is born of a woman is a few days and full of trouble." Such was my life, full of trouble. I was stuck on a road that was heading for a tragic life. It seemed I was an innocent victim of the generational sins of my family that the Bible makes reference to in the Old Testament. Numbers 14:18 "The Lord is longsuffering and forgiving iniquity and transgression, and by no means clearing the guilty, visiting the iniquity of the fathers upon the children unto the third and fourth generation." Truthfully we all are victims of generational sin that was passed down from Adam and Eve. It is called the curse of sin upon mankind which is traced back to Genesis chapter 3. Sad fact is we are all born with a sinful nature and trouble will come because of that.

A few years later my dad remarried a woman with two sons. It's never easy being part of a step family especially when you don't fit in. I had an older sister and a younger sister but now I had an older stepbrother and a younger stepbrother. I was still stuck in the middle again, the middle of a troubled life. My stepmother was not the most loving person I ever met. I'm sure marrying my dad wasn't so easy with him having three kids of his own. My youngest sister Mary and I moved to our "new home" but my oldest sister Cecelia stayed with my grandparents. When it came time for my oldest sister to get married, my dad refused to go to her wedding and refused to walk her down the aisle. My youngest sister and I were discouraged from attending the wedding. I really didn't know what the problem was but I think it had to do with our older sister not approving of our dad marrying this lady or not getting along with her. I wondered myself after a while who could get along with her. The heartbreak that my dad caused broke my grandfather Dominick's heart and really disturbed the rest of our family. Our family was a very close family. We had many family gatherings, but that soon changed after my dad isolated himself from his family. As the years went by I could not believe how he changed. We were a badly broken and troubled family. Was there any way for my sisters and me to find happiness anywhere? It seemed as if my life was cursed no matter where we were living and who we were with.

I started raiding my dad's liquor cabinet when I was in junior high school. I also had a large newspaper route that I did after school. It was a walking route in a large apartment complex in Tarrytown at the Tappan Landing apartments. They used to leave the newspapers at a certain street corner each day near the complex. I wonder if they still have those kinds of newspaper routes today. During my junior high years my stepmother would not allow me to go out for any after school sports. She complained that I might get hurt and not be able to work. When I was a freshman in high school I started smoking marijuana. One of my friends introduced me to it. I wasn't really a drug addict or pothead; I just started following the crowd. The alcohol and drugs were a way of escape from the problems at home. It was after the foot ball games and at the high school dances is when we would mess ourselves up with that junk. Also in my freshman year in high school I got interested in weightlifting. Finally I was able to get involved with sports at school. Soon weightlifting became the escape for me. I tried the wrestling team one year and broke my ankle in practice. I wondered if my step mom didn't jinx me then. I played football too and was privileged to be on the Sleepy Hollow Headless Horsemen football team. In 1972, my senior year, our team went undefeated and ended the season as the undefeated state champions.

I enjoyed playing football but my passion was always weight lifting and still is. Our school hosted a weightlifting meet with other schools my senior year. I only weighed 170lbs. at the time and was able to bench press 350lbs. Along with the military press and the leg squats I was the overall winner of that competition. The local newspaper referred to me as the Charles Atlas of the weight lifting meet. If they only knew how dead my soul and spirit was. If they only knew how much of a loser I felt I was.

Some of my childhood heroes were Steve Reeves, who played Hercules and Bruno Samartino who was the world wrestling heavyweight champion. In fact one year when I was about eight or nine year's old my dad took me to an outdoor wrestling match that featured Bruno Samartino against Cowboy Bill Watson. When we were walking into the arena I could hardly believe my eyes. There in front of me, walking towards me near an outdoor phone booth was Bruno. I went up to him, he greeted me and he shook my hand. I thought that was the greatest day of my life but that day would come in the summer of 1980 at my Aunt Helen's and Uncle Joe's farm house in Falls, Pennsylvania. Aunt Helen was my second mom. My sisters and I and some of our cousins would spend many of our summers at her house. We would have a lot of fun out there. My cousin Johnny and I drove out one year and had blast. My aunt would stay up and play board games with us all night long. My uncle Joe made the best pizza in the world. My dad thought this was a good place for us to be, away from our mom during the summer. There was no way that he could trust her with us when we were out of school. My mom had two sisters, Helen and Millie and two brothers Joseph and Raymond. Joseph had lost his life during war times in the Army. Being at my Aunt Helen's farm house in Pennsylvania was so different from being home in New York.

In the summer of my junior year in high school I reconnected with my mom. Thanks to a relative of my Aunt Millie. This relative's husband was the groundskeeper of the golf course I was caddying at, the Knollwood Country Club. I remember taking a bus from Tarrytown to White Plains the day that I was to meet up with my mom. When I walked into the restaurant where she worked tears began to flow from my eyes. When I walked in the door I saw her behind the counter waiting on someone. When she looked up and saw me coming she began to smile and cry at the same time. She came over to me and gave me the biggest hug that seemed to last forever. And I think she might've kissed me more than I can remember. She treated me to the best hot roast beef sandwich with french fries that I ever had. And I think she gave me the biggest hot fudge sundae on the planet. It was a very good day to spend some time with her; after all she was my real mom.

My mom was a very generous lady and she was an incredible cook. She was by far the best cook in our Italian family. Everybody loved her cooking and my two sisters take after her when it comes to cooking. After a few years my youngest sister Mary moved in with our mom. Things were getting very tense at home with our stepmother and my sister decided to leave. My mom wasn't drinking as much when my sister moved in with her. But sad to say she would have her bad days of drinking and battling depression. Studies show that most people who suffer from depression are because of sexual sin and guilt. One day I would get know why she was the way she was and why she was so self destructive.

My mom's apartment was located at 82 Bank Street in White Plains New York. What a place, what a neighborhood and what a setup. My mom had a job with the Salvation Army at the corner of her apartment complex. Everybody knew her as Miss Rose. I would soon discover that she was a fence, which is someone who receives and buys stolen property. People would come to her store and also come up to her apartment selling her everything from stolen jewelry to stolen filet mignons. Where she got the money to buy all these things I never knew, but I would soon find out. She wasn't making a lot of money working at the Salvation Army.

I would soon discover that my mother Rose was also a "double agent." She was an informant for the city police department and involved with the illegal numbers racket as well. This was long before the state run lotteries came to be legal. She would tip off her detective friend when the drug dealers were around the neighborhood. In the meantime she was the middle "guy" when it came to the illegal numbers that people would gamble on. My mom had some business going. Local bookies would come to her at a certain time of the day and drop off their numbers where she worked at the Salvation Army. She put them in an empty cigarette box that she would bring up to her apartment and hide them in a shower cap that was hanging in her bathtub. Later that day someone would come to her apartment and pick up the numbers. When my mom needed some extra money she would have one of her bookie friends leave a small space between two numbers so she can write the numbers in after they came out. It was three numbers that somehow involved some of the horse tracks I believe. I'm not really sure how that all worked but I know the odds were $500 to 1 when you hit the number. How this all happened was unbelievable to me.

When she wanted to hit the number she would call her detective friend and asked him to have a patrol car parked at the corner near her apartment building. This was his way of helping her after all she did for him in catching the drug dealers. When the patrol car was parked there the person picking up the numbers for my mom would not come to her apartment until the patrol car left. The police car would stay at the corner until my mom went upstairs and had time to write in the three numbers that had already come out. She would write these numbers in

7

the space that her bookie friend left for her. The person picking up the numbers at my mom's would never chance going there and getting caught while the police car was parked there. The police car did not leave until my mom called her detective friend to tell him that she was all set. She did not do this too often but when she did she hit the number for a lot of money. And you know she never got caught. When she did hit the number she was very generous.

In fact before I was a Christian I gambled a lot. I played blackjack at the casinos when they opened up and always won. I read two books on how to win at blackjack and followed their winning way. I even hit the number myself one day when I was playing the time that our first son was born. The day those numbers came out I happened to be at my mom's. She was thrilled to see me win, especially without her cheating the system. In fact I had put a bet on that number with her bookie friend for the whole week and hit it on the third day.

We had family members on both sides that were involved in organized crime. Some of my relatives married into organized crime families. One in particular was using their business as a front for a drug business. I had my opportunities to get involved but never did. I had my first real job at a gas station in Tarrytown New York. One year I was approached by this man called Danny. I was asked to be a partner in stealing very expensive men's suits. I did not want that kind of life for me especially after hearing how this guy's first partner we called "Wrong Way" dropped dead in a men's department store when he was stopped by a store detective trying to leave the store. In high school I was approached to sell marijuana with one of my friends and I refused. I guess I feared my dad too much or was it that someone, somewhere was praying for me.

I attended Rockland Community College for one semester when I got out of high school.

Later I transferred to Westchester Community College in Valhalla NY. During my final semester I was recruited by one of my college professors to do a summer internship with the Dobbs

8

Ferry Police department. I enjoyed overseeing the waterfront park for the summer located down by the Hudson River. One summer night I noticed some red flares being shot from what appeared to be a boat in trouble. I radioed the police station and reported a boat in distress on the river. They contacted the Coast Guard and in about thirty minutes they rescued the family that was stranded in the river. Apparently they ran out of gas. When this family was towed to shore they were told I was the one who saw them and was responsible for their rescue. They couldn't thank me enough, especially the children. That was a great night. I graduated from Westchester Community College with a degree in Criminal Justice in 1975. It was there where I met my wife Gayla. For me it was love at first sight. We were in the same English class together. It wasn't long before I got her phone number and was planning to take her out on a date.

The weekend I was supposed to call her to take her out I ended up landing in the hospital suffering from an appendix attack. Funny thing was I remembered that she told me that she worked in a hospital in our county somewhere but I wasn't really sure which one. When I was wheeled into my hospital room after surgery I asked the nurse if there was a young lady by the name of Gayla that worked there. To my surprise she said yes and told me that she was working downstairs in the kitchen that day. She was a dietitian there at Phelps Memorial Hospital where I ended up. Wow, was that not the coolest thing ever. It wasn't long until she came up to see me that day and well the rest is history. Man did she spoil me with the best meal trays in the hospital. I was getting very special treatment. Double portions of whatever I wanted to eat. By this time I no longer weighed 170 pounds like I did in high school. I was really into some heavy weightlifting and I weighed around 200 pounds. They say the best way to a man's heart is by his stomach. There might be some truth to that. Soon we started dating in March 1974, fell in love and got married in May of 1978.

I was fortunate to be able to purchase a home in Elmsford in August of 1977. It was a nice small cape cod that was priced at $48,000.00. My monthly mortgage payment was $214.00. I lived there alone until the day we were married. I'm glad we were old fashion in our ways. It was a great feeling to move out of my house and into my own home. At that time I was working at the General Motors assembly plant in North Tarrytown which was later renamed Sleepy Hollow. During my ten years there I worked mainly in the Plant Security Department. I did work in the Maintenance department as a temporary foreman covering vacations for a short time. Soon after I attended the G.M. Supervisory Training Classes and after graduation I soon was offered a position as a production foreman in the Body Shop that I accepted.

From the time I started working at G.M. in November of 1976 until August of 1980, I was not a Christian. In fact I was far from being a Christian. I was kind of religious being catholic and made sure we would go to church on the holidays. I was not aware that I was on a road the Bible refers to in Matthew 7:13 as "…broad is the way, that leadeth to destruction, and many there be which go in thereat:" I was a little religious but little did I know how lost I was. After I became a Christian in August of 1980, most of my coworkers at GM thought I was going through a phase in my life. They thought I would grow out of it but that never happened. Some people even thought I had lost my mind. I did lose my wicked mind to come to think of it. I became very dissatisfied with working in the production department mainly because some of the other foremen were involved in some illegal activity. Since I came from the Security Department some of them did not trust working with me. I just didn't fit in with this crowd. I also thought working in the body shop area in production was very unhealthy, smelling all those fumes and all.

I finally got a transfer back to the Security Department only to find myself in a real mess. One night people who were coming into work reported that there was a car on fire in our salary parking lot. You guessed it, it was mine. It was my 1978 white Monte Carlo that was on fire. Word had it that someone wanted to put a bomb in my car to get rid of me. I was devastated and terrified at the same time. I had a precious wife and three sons at home that I worried about. I was on edge for quite some time. I would always have a loaded gun ready in my house in case anyone tried to break in or come after me or my family. Trouble seems to find me no matter where I was. I never did find out who was responsible but I have a good idea and I know that God knows who did it. As time went on there were no more threats. Life seemed to calm down for a few years until I got involved in helping our security department try to organize a union with the Federation of Police Union. We were hearing that GM was going to contract out their security department and our jobs were in jeopardy. We also kept hearing that the plant was going to shut down. That finally did happen in June of 1996.

I volunteered to head up the union drive when asked. Brother did trouble come my way when I did that. GM brought in these people from Detroit, public relations specialists. They promised to take care of our problems and our problem supervisor that mostly everybody had a hard time with. This fellow thought he worked for the FBI in GM. He was the hardest guy get along with. The company did send him away to be retrained and when he returned he did calm down some. He would often go to a secret room behind our main lobby and connect into the telephone extensions of our security post, especially the chassis main gate. He would then listen in on our phone conversations. I would always know when he was in there listening to my phone conversations. I think he might've thought I was involved with the drug scene since someone in my family married into a family who dealt heavily with cocaine. One day this "family member" was set up by a girl that was selling for them who got busted by the police. She made a deal to get him to drive her to a hotel in their town where a man wanted to buy a very large quantity of cocaine. That man was an undercover detective. My friend went to jail for a long time for that and rightfully so, but he wasn't the one running the drug business, his brother was. He just did his brother a favor by delivering the drugs to the buyer. You know they say that crime does not pay. If you're going to play, one day you will have to pay. I call that the boomerang effect. What goes around comes around. The Bible refers to that as "reaping what you sow" in life.

The time came to have the vote for the union and we lost by a very small number. With all the security officers that said they would be voting yes it looked like we had no problem winning. Some obviously had changed their minds and we lost. I guess the guys from Detroit did their jobs. There was even a letter by G.M. that named me a troublemaker and suspected that three names might have been forged that might have been on the initial union cards. That was so far from the truth and I was surprised that I didn't take legal action against the one responsible for that letter. After the investigation, it was obvious that the accusation was false because none of the three men's names were on the initial union cards. In fact one of those men used to have a voice activated mini tape recorder in his pocket and was taping some of the security officers at their posts. He would get them to open up about things he wanted to bring to the attention of the chief. I saw the tape recorder one night on the desk at the body gate. I was tempted to take it and not give it back. While he was out checking on a truck outside I turned the tape recorder on and heard the voice of another security officer who he had just relieved an hour earlier at this post. I heard as much as I could before he was coming back to the post. At the end of the night I informed the other security officer of what I found and what I heard and cautioned him to be careful around this other security officer. I must say working there I was around many people who were the worst kind of backstabbers you can ever imagine. I call them "snakes in the grass."

I was coming up to my ten years of service with G.M. in November of 1986. The company began offering buyouts to the salaried employees around that same time. I began praying about taking that buy out package because I was sensing that my future would GM was probably over. I soon found myself at a crossroads in my life. Do I stay here at GM as a marked man or do I leave with ten years of vested service and take the buyout? I had much peace about leaving GM. In fact that same week I was reading in an article in a Christian magazine about the blessings of leaving with a severance package when God is leading you to. They illustrated it by comparing a bird in a cage that had the door opened for him to fly out. The door was not only opened for him to fly out but the bird was able to take a good amount of seed with him for his journey. I knew it was time for me to go. It was time to "fly the coop."

One night while I was working in the receiving room a material department employee ran over my right foot with his transport truck. I don't know how he could not have seen me and I wondered if it was not intentional. Fortunately I was with another security officer at the time that was able to transport me to the local hospital for treatment. My foot was swollen and turned black, blue and yellow. The x-rays showed no broken bones and soon I was released to go home. I did see our family doctor the next day he told me to stay off it for a few days and gave me some medication. He told me not to go to work and put any pressure on it for a few days. A couple of days later my foot was feeling a little better so I took my three sons to the playground to give my wife some quiet time. What I didn't know was that GM had someone watching me at my house from up the street in a park car. When I left with my three boys's my wife got a call from a security supervisor asking to speak to me. She told him that I was upstairs sleeping and she would have me call them back later. She was scared to tell them the truth about where I was. She was trying to protect me. It is never right to be dishonest even with good intentions. After a short time she wrote me a note and taped it to the front door for me to see when I got home since she was leaving the house for a while. This was 1986 when we did not have any cell phones.

When I got home that late afternoon I got a very uneasy feeling when I read that note on the front door. I sensed that

13

someone else might have read that letter. After reading the letter I called my supervisor at work to return his call. He informed me that the personnel director wanted to see me the next day in his office. I had a feeling that was not good news. The next day was a rough one but a true blessing in disguise. I was confronted with what happened the day before. I was told that they had someone from personnel relations come to my house and they saw the note on the door and read it. That person then reported that information back to my supervisor and the personnel director. It wasn't long before the plant manager came into the office and joined the meeting. When I was threatened with termination I began to weep. I asked to be excused to the restroom to compose myself and the plant manager followed me in there. While I was washing my face and trying to get myself together the plant manager came next to me and was very sensitive about what was going on. I told him I'll be fine in a few minutes and he went back out in the meeting room with the personnel director. I was thinking about taking off my shoe and sock on my bruised foot and showing them how black and blue it still was.

When I returned to the room there was a peace that had come over me, a peace that passes all understanding. It was the peace of God flooding my soul in the midst of a troubled storm that I found myself in. When I sat down I was told that they had some good news for me. They were able to offer me a special ten year buyout package instead. This would also include an all expense paid trip to Troy, Michigan where I would attend a four day career workshop. After I shed a few more tears I realized my career with GM was over and I signed the papers for the ten year buyout. Thank God! The moment I left the parking lot I was relieved knowing that the Lord was with me and He has never let me down. When I got home I shared the news with my wife who was very upset about what happened because she felt totally responsible. The next thing I know that night I was taking her out to dinner to celebrate a new direction for our life. That night I did receive a few phone calls from some

14

of my fellow officers who wanted to know what happened. I told them that they threatened to fire me but I took the buyout when they offered it to me and I was very happy. I have to say that there is life after General Motors.

I enjoyed those four days at the career workshop and learned a great deal. I landed a job with a large security company that provided security for I.B.M. I was now a security supervisor overseeing several I.B.M. buildings and many employees. Yes there is life after General Motors and a blessed life at that. I had worked for several different companies from the time I left GM in 1986. They were some big companies with great paying jobs and good benefits. The company's I worked for were: Coca Cola as a production supervisor and the quality control supervisor, Federal Express as a driver and customer service agent. I even was approached by the hiring manager of I.B.M. who offered me a position in their security department. What an honor. It seemed every job I interviewed for I landed. I tried them all. I worked for the Pennysaver in advertising. That was short lived after someone's wife who worked at G.M. told the management about me being a "trouble making union guy". I also worked in a car dealership selling cars for a short while, but wasn't able to sell many cars to make a good living. It wasn't long before that place went out of business. I even had my own business for a while; a convenience store inside a friend's gas station in Tarrytown called "Teddy's Pit Stop." In fact it was the same gas station I worked at while I was in high school. I must say that one of the best jobs I had was actually my last one while I lived in N.Y. I was working for the Town of Greenburg in the Parks and Recreation department. It was great to enjoy a good paying job with great benefits with no stress and it was also close to home.

In the beginning of the summer of 1990 the Lord began to work in my heart about serving Him in full time ministry. For the longest time I had such a desire to share the message of salvation to whoever crossed my path. No matter where I worked my heart was fixed in sharing the gospel of Jesus

Christ to anyone and everyone I met. One Sunday morning we watched a video of a testimony of an Evangelist named David Ring in our Sunday school class at our church in Elmsford. Brother Ring's words were powerful and God used this man who had cerebral palsy to speak to my heart. My heart broke as I surrendered to do God's will for my life. That Sunday was a turning point in my life at Grace Baptist Church in Elmsford, N.Y. As I watched and listened to David Ring's testimony, his words and the Word of God were reaching my heart. When he said," I have cerebral palsy, what's your problem healthy people?" my heart was broken with conviction. The Lord had been dealing with me for sometime about giving Him my life in full time ministry. I surrendered to do His will. I wonder have you surrendered to do God's will yet?

It was about two years later when I made plans to go to Bible College in Jacksonville Florida. That would mean selling our house, quitting my job and leaving our families. We placed our house for sale by owner with a homemade sign in the front yard. About the same time my mom was admitted to the hospital after one of her dialysis treatments. A few years back she almost died when her kidneys were failing. All that alcohol had finally destroyed her kidneys. Here is a fact, alcohol is poison. The Bible is very clear about alcohol. Proverbs 23:29-35 is where you find what God says about it. In verse 32 we read: "At the last it biteth like a serpent, and stingeth like an adder." It sure did poison my mom and our family. God also has a warning label that should be on every alcoholic beverage. 1 Corinthians 6:9, 10 "Be not deceived: no drunkards…shall inherit the kingdom of God." There needs to be warning labels like they have on tobacco products. They warn you of getting lung cancer and the one I like the best just says, "GOVERNMENT WARNING: SMOKING KILLS.' Why can't that warning label be on every can and bottle of alcohol? It certainly needs to be. Alcohol destroys lives and ruins families. In fact a deacon at our church, Brother Carl, sent me a picture of a warning label on an alcoholic beverage at a store in Myrtle Beach he noticed while he was on a family vacation this year. That should be mandatory nationwide.

I would soon find out that my mom's condition was very critical. The doctors informed me that she had advanced cancer of the pancreas and the liver. They said there was nothing they could do but keep her comfortable because they did not expect her to live very long. It wasn't long until I got a call about our house for sale around the same time. This couple called and told me they were driving by our house and wanted to see it. They came over that afternoon and fell in love with the house and made us an offer. I accepted and the process began. What they said to me blew me away. They told me that they prayed in front of my house and that God gave them peace about buying this house even before they even stepped inside. I was speechless about what the Lord was doing. I remembered praying while I put that sign in our yard, "Lord Jesus please help us sell this house so I can follow your will."

One night while I was sitting by her bedside in her hospital room my mom shared her heart with me. For almost 50 years she kept a deep dark secret locked in her soul. This dark secret caused many of the problems of her life. She shared with me that when she was a teenager her father had sexually molested her many times. There was even a time when this wicked man wanted to run away with her. All these years she was afraid to open up and tell her story like so many other people in the world today. She never told anyone what happened because she was afraid and ashamed like most people who have shared similar experiences. She had much pain in her life because of him. She always thought when she lost her twin sons at birth that God was punishing her for her sins of the past with her father. The experience of losing her newborns at birth was devastating to her and my father. My twin brothers were born two years before me in 1953. One day I'll get to meet them in heaven.

That night in the hospital I held my mom as she wept and as she relived those dark days of the past. All these years she was a prisoner until that night. Is there anything in your past that's keeping you a prisoner? I was trying to comfort her about the forgiveness of God, His mercy and His grace. One of the first people in my family that I shared the good news of salvation in Christ Jesus was with my mom. I remember several years before I had led her to the Lord. She stopped drinking and stopped the pills but she kept on smoking two packs of cigarettes a day. I spent a long time that night in the hospital with her, loving on her and wiping away her tears. Before I left that night I kissed her and I told her I loved her. These were the last words I heard my mom say to me, "son I love you and please pray for me". I told her that I would and that I would see her the next day, but God had other plans. She passed away the next day which was a Sunday, July 12,1992 at about 6:00am. When it came time for the funeral arrangements my sisters and I all agreed on a beautiful light pink casket with a lovely rose decoration on it.

The week of her funeral so many thoughts went through my mind. One disturbing thought was about her dad, Rocco, and how wicked he was. All the struggles my mom had to deal with all those years and how she was afraid to tell anyone. The guilt of her past was destroying her life. Looking back on her life now I understand why she battled depression, why the drinking and why the suicide attempts. It was a cry for help. I was so blessed to be with her the last two weeks of her life, especially the last night of her life. My thoughts went back to my twin brothers that she lost at birth. How difficult that must've been for her. Then I realized something that I never shared with anyone else. Something I was very ashamed of concerning my dad.

When I was a junior in high school I was over one of my friend's house when his mother shared something with me that overwhelmed me. As I was sitting at her kitchen table eating some of her freshly made meatballs I'll never forget what she said to me. It was like a sword had cut into my heart. She asked me if I knew that my father use to help girls get abortions when she was back in high school. I was speechless. I was in shock.

18

I lost my appetite. I told her I did not know anything about that and soon I got up and walked outside to wait for her son. Then when I got home that night I was very quiet and did not say anything to my dad about what I was told. For several weeks it really bothered me until one afternoon when he and I were sitting on our couch watching a football game together, I asked him about it. Up to that time I kind of refused to believe it. I always respected my dad for being a hardworking man and having a great reputation as a master carpenter. I was very proud of the fact that the governor of New York, Nelson Rockefeller, who was also the Vice President for short time, hired him and my two uncles, Bill and George, to oversee the construction of a very expensive Japanese tea house that Rockefeller had constructed for his wife Happy on their estate.

I told my dad I needed to ask him a very important question. So I asked him about what my friend's mom told me. The room was very quiet for a little while and then he looked at me and said it was true. He said that my uncle Benny from Bayonne would pose as the doctor and my father would set up these back alley abortions for them. I couldn't believe that, I didn't want to believe that but it was true. There wasn't much conversation after that and after the football game was over I left to go out. I was really brokenhearted and realized what a messed up family I had. I was ashamed and very confused about life. Have you ever felt that way?

Two weeks after we buried my mom, we closed on our house that we sold in Elmsford. I hired a mover and my wife and I packed as much as we could in the 1984 Buick Skyhawk and headed to Jacksonville Florida with our three sons. The moving company told us it would be five days before they got to our rental home in Florida because they had another small stop on the way. We had several suitcases packed that we had strapped to the roof rack on our car. We also packed as much as we could in our trunk. We were excited about the journey and the new life a head of us in Florida.

The five day journey down the East Coast was great. We made stops at Wildwood New Jersey, Virginia Beach, Myrtle Beach, and Savannah Georgia and finally we made it to Jacksonville Florida in July of 1992. We were able to stay in some really nice Courtyards at each stop thanks to my sister Cecelia who gave me a great discount since she worked for Marriot at the time. We settled in at our rental home and a few days later I took the family to Orlando on a much needed vacation before school would start in August. My wife Gayla soon got a job at the Christian school where our sons attended. She was working in the school cafeteria. My first job was a part time position telemarketing for a local newspaper. The first few months went well as we all enjoyed life in Jacksonville Florida. This was going to be a much better life than the life I had in New York, or was it?

One night in October when I came home from work my wife looked very upset. My boys were already in bed asleep. She could not wait to tell me about her day. The local news station happened to be in front of our house that afternoon and my wife was curious as to why. The reporter came over to my wife who was in our front yard and asked her about living across the street from our neighbor. She had no idea why she was being asked that because we were new to the area and really didn't know too much about our neighbors. It seemed like a very nice neighborhood. The news reporter told my wife that the man who lives directly across the street from us was suspected of murdering his wife and possibly burying her somewhere in the subdivision. I was in shock when I heard this. The reporter said our neighbor's wife went missing since September of 1991. My wife looked at me with a very intense look and said we lived in New York for all these years and never had this kind of a problem. Now you move us here across the street from a murderer. She said she wanted to go back home to New York. I couldn't blame her, I was ready myself to leave after hearing that.

Why is it, no matter where I am, trouble seems to find me. Florida was no different than NY. I promised her that we would move as soon as possible and I quickly called our rental agent and told him that we would be moving soon because of the neighbor across the street. I always wondered why he never told me about this fellow, I guess renting the house was more important to him. We did move to another subdivision but not before my car was stolen from our driveway one night. This was in December of 1992, during final exam week in Bible College. Like I needed more stress on me during finals week. It was around 5:30 in the morning when I heard a knock on the door. When I opened the door a police officer asked me if I was Theodore Ricci and I said yes I was. He asked me if I owned a 1987 Cavalier station wagon and of course I said I did. He then informed me that my car was stolen and if I could come with him to the vehicle. I was already dressed because at that time I would be up around four in the morning praying and studying for school. I had a feeling this was not going to be a good day. Driving over to the scene the officer asked me if I had any enemies in town. I told him I didn't think so. There was no one that I knew of that I had a problem with. I was new here and I was a Bible college student studying for the ministry. He told me that when we got to the vehicle I could check and see if there was anything worth keeping since the car also was set on fire and was destroyed. I was in complete shock. What in the world was going on now?

Will my life get any better? I thought I was on the right road to find true peace and happiness in the will of God. Did I make the wrong turn when I found myself at a crossroads in my life back to New York? I soon found out that there was an organized crime family in the area with the same last name as mine. This was not what I needed now, more trouble. I had this same problem when I first moved into my house in Elmsford New York. I received phone calls at all hours of the night asking me if I was related to someone from that town with the same last name as mine. Each time I would tell them the truth that I wasn't related to him and I didn't even know the man. One thing was for sure when I was in some of the stores in town I would receive really big discounts and special treatment just because of my last name. Here we are over a thousand miles away from New York and I still have trouble finding me no matter where I am.

When we got to my car it was scary to realize what happened again. Another car torched and destroyed. This time the car was stolen as well. I opened the trunk and saw that the kids had some baseball stuff in there as well as some of their Game Boys. Everything in the car was ruined. I signed some papers for the officer to have my car towed and he drove me back home. I got back home just in time to have prayer with my very upset family and head off to school. What a day this turned out to be. The next morning we found out there were several cars stolen out of our subdivision. We also found out there were a few houses that were broken into. It seemed that a street gang had an initiation night for new members and they picked our subdivision. Our next door neighbor told me that his truck in his driveway was tampered with. It seemed they tried to steal it and couldn't so they came next door and stole my car from my driveway. The following week we went shopping for a used vehicle and we purchased a used 1993 Ford Aerostar van. We really enjoyed it; we ended up getting over 270,000 miles on it before I bought another used vehicle.

It wasn't too long before our family was in our new home away from the problem neighborhood where we first moved into. I was shocked to hear that the neighbor who was the murder suspect was arrested and later pleaded guilty to third degree murder of his adoptive mother. He ended up on death row. I once gave him a gospel tract and asked him to read it one night. He would always come out at night to walk his dog who somehow found his way into my home one night when we came home from church. It was the strangest thing when that dog ran into my house, turned down the hallway and ended up in my bedroom. He sat down and stared up at my dresser. I had a gospel tract on the dresser called Bad Bob that I took to give to our neighbor. I was standing in my room looking down at that dog and I prayed "Lord if you want me to give this tract to this man I will." Sure enough as soon as I picked that tract up that dog turned and headed out of my front door to the front yard. I handed our neighbor that tract and told him I believed the Lord wanted him to read it. This was a month before we knew he was suspected of murdering his wife. That was the last time I ever saw him.

My four years at Trinity Baptist College in Jacksonville Florida seem to take forever. I started there when I was 37 years old with my wife and three sons. Jason was 11, Sean 9, and Justin was 7. Graduation day finally came in May of 1996. I was thankful that the Lord blessed me with a great part time job with ADT my last two years of school. In fact I was able to get many of our college student's jobs there. Now it was time for me to serve the Lord full time. I could not believe where the Lord was about to send my family and I. Now at 41 years old there was another new road that God would direct me on. I had accepted a position of Associate Pastor at the Community Baptist Church in Franklin Ohio. How in the world did we go from New York to Jacksonville Florida and now to Franklin Ohio?

Looking back I could see that our destination was all mapped out for us as I followed the Lord's direction for our family. I can truly say that leaving General Motors was one of the best things that ever happened to me. It helped me to really focus on following God's direction at that crossroad in my life. We will all come to a crossroad in our life at sometime or another. Looking back now I understand more of what Isaiah wrote: "For my thoughts are not your thoughts, neither are your ways my ways, saith the LORD. For as the heavens are higher than the earth, so are my ways higher than your ways, and my thoughts than your thoughts." Isaiah 55:8,9. Ok Lord, Ohio here we come, please help us as we follow Your will for our lives.

Chapter Two

"LOOKING AROUND"

———————— ∞∞∞ ————————

As I look around my church office I can't help but to be in
awe of how the Lord directed my family and me here in
Ohio. I am often so humbled by the call of God in my life to
be the senior pastor of our church here in Germantown, First
Baptist Church. This journey began at the Dutchess County
fair in Rhinebeck New York. It was the summer of 1980 when
my wife and I were enjoying the fair and especially the food.
After a while we walked over to listen to a group playing some
music under a large white tent. It wasn't long before this group
ended their last song and I sensed an unusual peace under that
tent. This was a gospel group singing a song about Jesus. This
song was one that we were not familiar with but most of the
crowd if not all of the crowd there seemed to know it as they
sang along. The words of this song began to touch my heart in
a way I had never known before. They were singing about the
love of God and the cross of Jesus. After a short time enjoying
that last song, my wife and I made our way to my car, a 1970
SS 350 Camaro, and we headed home.

For several weeks I kept thinking about that experience
under that tent and the song they were singing about Jesus.
Finally one night I called my Aunt Helen, who was like my
second mom, and began to share with her that I thought God

was trying to get my attention. She was the first person in our family to become a born again Christian. Truthfully at first we all thought this "new religion" of hers was just a little too much. I was too curious now about what was going on in my heart and I needed some answers. She invited my wife and I out to her house in Falls Pennsylvania to spend the night and attend a home Bible study at her house that Thursday night. It just so happened that my days off for that week were Thursday and Friday. So Pennsylvania here we come. I believe it was on that Thursday night, August 7th, 1980 when my life would never be the same.

That afternoon we arrived at my Aunts house and enjoyed some of my Uncle Joe's homemade pizza. I still say his pizza was the best on the planet by far. It wasn't long before people began to arrive at her house and her family room filled up with those who came to the Bible study. I would say that there were at least 20 or more people who were there. It wasn't long before we began to sing some gospel hymns of praise to the Lord. At the end of the last song we concluded in prayer and a man opened his Bible and began the devotion on the grace of God. I didn't have a Bible; in fact I never even owned one. To come to think of it, I never even wanted to open a Bible before. At the end of his lesson this man shared the gospel of Jesus Christ and asked if there was anyone there who desired to turn their life over to the Lord and be saved. He explained verse by verse (which I will do in a later chapter) that we are all sinners separated from God and hell was our final destination without Christ. Now up to that point in my life I knew stories about Jesus. I can remember when I was young that I wept when I watched the movie; "The King of Kings" that starred Jeffery Hunter as Jesus. But now I found myself at crossroads in my life. I was confronted with a Bible truth concerning my eternal destiny. There was a choice that was now before me that would determine my future. Do I stay on the road that I am on which is leading me to place called hell? I knew I was a terrible sinner and if anyone deserved hell it was me.

I soon indicated, by the raising of my hand, that I wanted to be saved. I wanted to turn to Jesus Christ and receive Him as my Lord and Savior. I needed His forgiveness and desired His gift of eternal life, the promise of heaven. I remember bowing my head and praying to the Lord. Soon after my prayer it was like something evil had left me and this awesome peace of God flooded my soul. I soon began to weep like I never wept before. This "joy unspeakable and full of glory" from heaven came and filled my heart. This truly was the greatest day of my life. That day I experienced the love and grace of God through Jesus Christ. I soon began my journey on a new road that would lead me to the writing of this book that you are now reading.

The next day as my wife and I drove back home to New York, I stopped at a Christian Bookstore in White Plains and purchased my first Bible. I asked the kind gentleman behind the counter about what Bible to get. I told him I was a new Christian and I had never owned a Bible before. He reached to the bookshelf behind him and handed me a King James Bible which I bought. I was a "baby Christian", new in the faith and being raised a catholic all my life I had some questions about the Bible. We hardly ever went to church, only on the holidays. I can't ever remember anyone who brought a Bible to church when we did go. We were never encouraged to bring one. We would read out of a booklet in the pews which contained some Bible passages during church. I don't think I ever really paid much attention about church back in those days.

After about a week or so I began to doubt all that had happened to me. I questioned my new found faith and was troubled. I remember reaching for my bible and opening it up at random. My eyes fell on John 3:18, a scripture I had never seen before. That bible verse reads: "He that believeth on him (meaning Jesus) is not condemned: but he that believeth not is condemned already, because he hath not believed in the name of the only begotten Son of God." I believe with all of my heart that God directed me to open to that exact passage in the gospel of John. I thought much about what had happened in

27

my life and my family up to this time. I came to realize that it was not about a religion it was about a relationship with the Son of God, Jesus Christ. Now by the blessed Holy Spirit and the Word of God, my new journey in life was to begin. It is such a comfort to know that God promises to supply all of our needs. This is especially true when it comes to looking around for directions to follow in your life. Just remember: Where the Lord directs you, He will protect you! Where the Lord guides you, He provides for you! Sounds great to me!

Let me share with you some amazing experiences I had with the Lord as He directed my life. One summer night after we had a birthday party for our son Jason, Gayla and I were in the kitchen cleaning up while our boys, Jason who had just turned two and Sean who was only four months old, were asleep. I was struggling with the fact that some of our relatives got a little drunk at the party at our house. We had some wine and beer that some of our family brought over that night to celebrate with. I was a young Christian at that time and I was not really sure about where I stood on "recreational drinking" at the family parties. As my wife and I were finishing up the dishes I shared with her about how unsettled I was about the drinking at our house. I was not comfortable with the alcohol at our house anymore. She agreed with me as well. As I was placing something back in the refrigerator I noticed I had placed my Bible on top of the refrigerator. I grabbed my Bible and just opened it up and began to read from the very first verse that my eyes fell to.

As I began to read the words on that page I knew that the very God of heaven was speaking directly to me by His Holy Word. I could not believe what I was directed to turn to in the Bible. There was no way that this just happened by chance or as some may say it was just a coincidence. How could I have opened my Bible to this portion of scripture without some Divine guidance! I was reading from the Old Testament book of Habakkuk in chapter 2 verse 15 which read: "Woe unto him that giveth his neighbor drink, that putteth thy bottle to him and maketh him drunken also..." This was unbelievable. I quickly called my wife back into the kitchen and shared with her what just happened. I read that verse to her and she stood there speechless. We were both kind of in shock and in utter amazement about what the Lord just did. He knew our hearts and about how we were feeling. God knew the struggle we were having with the booze at our home. He was directed us by His Word to confirm that He was not pleased with it either. So now what do we do. My wife and I looked at each other and we both realized it was time to rid our home of all the alcohol.

We soon found ourselves downstairs in our basement where we emptied all of the bottles of alcohol down the laundry sink. What a joy and peace we experienced as we followed the Lord's direction and His way. In the book of Proverbs, the book of wisdom, King Solomon writes: "Wine is a mocker, strong drink is raging: and whosoever is deceived thereby is not wise." (Proverbs 20:1) There is another great portion of scripture dealing with alcohol found in Proverbs 23:29-33 "Who hath woe? Who hath sorrow? Who hath contentions? Who hath babbling? Who hath wounds without cause? Who hath redness of eyes? They that tarry long at the wine; they that go to seek mixed wine. Look not thou upon the wine when it is red, when it giveth colour in the cup, when it moveth itself aright. At last it biteth like serpent, and stingeth like an adder. Thine eyes shall behold strange woman, and thine heart shall utter perverse things." Simply the Bible says that alcohol is poison to your body and to your family. It ruins lives just like drugs do. In fact just one drink begins to affect every organ in your body.

As I matured as a Christian I developed a strong faith in the Word of God. There is no doubt in my mind that this ancient G.P.S. (God's Perfect Scriptures and God's Preserved Scriptures) is from heaven to help guide our steps in life. Here are a few other G.P.S.'s from heaven: God's Plan of Salvation, God's Promised Savior, God's Precious Son and God's Powerful Spirit. I have experienced God's supernatural direction in my life many times, especially when I found myself at a crossroads. Here are some of those experiences that I was so blessed with as I sought the Lord for His help in my life.

While I was attending Bible College in Jacksonville Florida, I was notified that I was eligible for a $5,500.00 Stafford Loan. This loan would not have to be paid back until a few months after I would graduate from Bible College in 1996. The payments would be at a very low interest rate which seemed to me like a great idea. The deadline to either accept or decline this loan was soon approaching. I was praying every day seeking God's direction about this loan. It came to the final day of decision when I found myself on my knees once again. The place where I was reading in my morning Bible devotions was in the Old Testament book of Deuteronomy. I was reading Deuteronomy 14, as I finished that chapter I felt lead to continue reading the next chapter. This was a prayer I was asking the Lord before I started reading Deuteronomy 15: "Lord Jesus should I borrow this money, should I take out this loan, please show me your will Lord, Amen." As I read chapter fifteen, I came across versus 5 and 6 which were words from God that He gave me that day. "Only if thou carefully hearken unto the voice of thy God, to observe to do all these commandments which I command thee this day. For the Lord thy God blesseth thee, as he promised thee:... But thou shall not borrow..." I was once again in the state of shock and blessed beyond measure as I read those words over and over again. The God of heaven himself gave me divine direction from his Word. I just read from God's Positional System which is God's Perfect Scriptures! The Holy Bible is our GPS for life.

It would not be until I graduated from Bible College and moved to Ohio that I would understand why God commanded me not to borrow that money and take out that Stafford loan. When I came to the school that day I went to the finance office to see Mrs. Harris. She was waiting for me with the loan papers. The peace of God that I had in my heart and the joy of the Lord that was flooding my soul that morning were hard to explain. Knowing that God gave me direction on this decision put such confidence in my mind as I walked up to meet with Mrs. Harris. I explained to her why I was declining the loan. I shared with her the verses that God gave me that morning after I was seeking His will concerning this decision. She was so amazed at the direct and specific answer that I received from God's Word that day. I cannot help not getting emotional when I think that the very God of heaven, the same God that spoke to Moses on the mountain, the same God who parted the great Red Sea, the same God who delivered Daniel out of the lion's den and the same God who was with Joseph during his troubled life, is the same awesome God that spoke to me by His inspired Word. He wants to speak to you too.

We are all on a journey to the Promised Land, which is the place of God's will for your life. In Exodus 13:21, 22 "And the Lord went before them by day in a pillar of a cloud, to lead them the way, and by night in a pillar of fire, to give them light; to go by day and night: He took not away the pillar of the cloud by day, nor the pillar of fire by night, from the people." We need to remember that where the Lord directs us He will protect us. When you follow God's will for your life you are blessed with Divine protection. I can truly say just as God was directing and protecting Moses and the children Israel on their journey to the Promise Land, He will do the same for you as He did for me. There was no doubt in my mind that the Lord was directing me not to take out that school loan. He was directing me to protect me from a financial disaster that I would've been in if I did take the $5,500.00 Stafford loan. Little did I know but God sure did, that after our family moved from Jacksonville Florida to Franklin Ohio that our house in Florida would not sell until some five months later.

It was a little difficult for us when we first arrived in Ohio being paid only $400.00 per week. Paying the rent on the place in Franklin and paying the mortgage and other expenses for our Florida home was rough. It would've been a financial disaster if I would've had to start paying on that Stafford loan as well.

We were just barely making it week by week anyway on what I was making. I know in my heart that the ancient GPS, the Bible, is how the Lord directed me and protected me from making a bad decision in borrowing that money. There was also a man at our church in Franklin that would hand me an envelope on some Sundays. He would tell me that the Lord put our family on his heart and he wanted to be a blessing to us. Oh man was he a blessing to us. The weeks that the finances weren't looking too good would be the same weeks that J.D. would hand me an envelope with some money it for our family. What a Mighty God we serve. Psalm 23:1 "The Lord is my shepherd I shall not want." I believe that your life will be very satisfied when you follow the Shepherd and trust Him. The money in that envelope was exactly what we needed for the groceries that week. J.D. would continue being a blessing to us for about the first year that we were in our new church.

Our family was truly being blessed by God just like He promised us that He would. You know that God never goes back on His promises to us. I've been disappointed by some people in my life but I never been disappointed by the Lord. A lot of people like to claim the promises of God but fail to meet the conditions to enjoy those promises. The conditions are an obedient heart and a surrendered will to the Lord. Now if I would've taken out that loan that payment would've been due starting with the month we had moved to Ohio. The financial strain on us would've been too much to handle. Praise the Lord for His direction in our lives. When we find ourselves at a crossroads in our life always be mindful that where God directs you He will protect you. Where the Lord guides you he will provide for you. God's protection and His provisions are what He promises to those who put their faith and trust in Him. It's not about our way, our will or what we want. It has to be God's way, God's will and what He desires for us.

Before He went to the cross to suffer and die for the sins of the world, Jesus was in the garden of Gethsemane praying: Matthew 26:39 "And he went a little further, and fell on his face, and prayed, saying, O my Father, if it be possible, let this cup pass from me nevertheless not as I will, but as thou wilt." The cup of suffering that Jesus was about to take for the human race was before Him. The cup meant a horrific death for Jesus for the sins of man. The cup would be the cross, a place of suffering and shame. The cross was a place of darkness, a place where He would be forsaken by the Father because of our sin. Jesus is our ultimate example to follow concerning our praying for the will of God to be done in our lives. That's why it's so important not to be swayed into making a decision especially when your emotions will most likely cause you to do something that you "feel good" about at the moment. Don't base your choices on your feelings because most of the time you will regret it afterwards. God will help you "if" you let Him! He knows what is best for you.

Our house in Florida finally sold in late December of 1996. In January of 1997 I told my "angel" J.D. that our family was in better financial shape now that we sold the house. I also told him he no longer needed to give me anything like he did before. I thanked him for his faithfulness in allowing God to use him in a great way in my life. I also told him how much of a blessing he was to me and my family. He said I was the one who was the blessing in his life and in our church here in Ohio.

You're probably wondering by now how we ended up moving to Franklin Ohio. I was in my senior year in Bible College when the Lord used a great man of God in my life. One morning right before my Advanced Theology class began my teacher Charles Shafer asked me if I knew what I was going to do when I graduated that year. Brother Shafer asked me if I had a desire to pastor a church. I told him that I felt I wasn't ready yet to pastor but I was open to more of an associate pastor position. I felt I needed more training and that a second man (associate pastor) was where I could serve best for awhile. He smiled as he reached into his front right pocket and handed me a piece of paper with a pastor's name and phone number. He said that right before he came upstairs to our class that he had received a call from a pastor in Franklin Ohio that was looking to hire an associate pastor. Brother Shafer then shared with me that the Lord had impressed upon his heart to give this ministry opportunity to me. He said that I would have to pray and seek the Lord for His will concerning this church.

When I got home from school I shared with my wife about what transpired that day. We both began to pray to the Lord for His direction and His wisdom. I called the pastor the next day and we spoke for quite sometime about ministry. He arranged for an interview during spring break in Jacksonville since he was coming with his nephew, who was a freshman at my college. He asked for a resume and I sent him one. You will never guess where we had the interview when he came down three months later in April. Are you ready for this? In my home that's where. That was a little awkward and unusual to say the least. My wife and I had prepared a big lunch for the Ohio crowd of 7 plus our 5. The interview went well and I was offered the position after we prayed together. I told the pastor that I would have to come and visit the church. Then I would need to seek the Lord for at least two weeks after that before I would give him an answer. The answer would be the direction that I would get from the Lord.

In June of 1996 our family drove up to Franklin Ohio. I was scheduled to meet with the pastor and the men of the church after the Sunday evening service. On Sunday morning I was asked to fill in to teach an adult Sunday school class for a teacher who had a family emergency. The Lord had me ready; in fact we are always to be ready to be used of the Lord at any time. I preached the Sunday morning service as well and seen many people come to the altar to pray when the service was closing. Sunday evening before I preached I met with the men of the church and the pastor. We had a time of prayer together and a time where I was asked many questions about ministry. While we were closing that session in prayer, I sensed the presence of God in that small room. We had another good service Sunday evening with another good response by the church members and visitors. When it was time for us to leave Ohio and continue our trip to New York, I informed the pastor that I would be praying for the next two weeks about God's will about me and my family coming to Ohio. This looked like a great opportunity to accept this Associate Pastor position at the Community Baptist Church in Ohio. Honestly I was not really crazy about the idea of moving to Ohio because some of the people at the church seemed to resent me being there. I could usually read people pretty well and the Lord did bless me with the gift of discernment. I did promise to pray for the Lord's will not mine so for the nest two weeks that's what our family did.

As my family and I approached the Tappan Zee Bridge in New York, driving from Rockland County over to Westchester County, the excitement was building as we were getting closer to home. Our kids couldn't wait to see our family back in New York. It was a great ride as we got onto the bridge with an awesome view of the Hudson River, the Kingsland Point Park Lighthouse and the General Motors plant by the river where I worked for ten years. Several years later as we made this same trip to visit family in New York I was stunned at what was missing on the Tarrytown–Sleepy Hollow side of the river. What was missing was the General Motors plant. My soul the entire plant was gone. All the buildings were gone. I could hardly believe what I was not seeing! I was wondering where in the world that huge factory went to. Did they tear down this plant and sell it as scrap? Am I sure blessed to have taken the early buyout when I did! Amen!

I think back now on how awesome the ways of the Lord are. Here it was June of 1996 and the G.M. plant was shut down. I had graduated from Bible College and now I was praying about a position in full time ministry in Ohio. I had a whole new life just like God promised. The timing was just a God Thing! My life was being guided each step of the way by Divine direction. We were about to start a new chapter in our lives.

Our time with our family in New York was wonderful but way too short as always. There's nothing like spending time with those that you love. Each day my wife and I spent much time in prayer seeking the Lord's will concerning Ohio. When we arrived back in Florida I began to fast and pray the final few days before the Lord would reveal to me His will. How crazy is this that now it seemed that everyday as I would be driving to work at ADT I would find myself behind a vehicle that had, you guessed it, an Ohio license plate. I would notice Ohio plates on trucks, cars and even motorcycles everyday. That weekend before the two week time period was coming to a close another "strange thing" occurred. My son's and I were playing catch in the back yard when I noticed on all the baseball equipment the name "Franklin." In fact even my baseball glove had "Franklin" on it. Was this another "sign" from God like all the Ohio license plates I've been seeing everyday? Did this name just supernaturally appear on my glove? I don't think so. It was there all along but I really never paid much attention until now. Why haven't I noticed that before? Why the name "Franklin?" And why now?

The day finally arrived that I would hopefully get an answer from the Lord. It was a Sunday and it was exactly two weeks prior that we visited Community Baptist Church (which has been renamed Mission Lane Baptist) in Franklin Ohio. I was to call the pastor the next day, on that Monday morning, to give him my decision. Do I accept this Associate Pastor position? Do I move my family to Ohio? Ohio, what in the world is in Ohio? Do I just wait for something else to come along? All these questions would soon be answered, besides it wasn't for me to decide. God would! I knew in my heart that the Lord would show me His will and His way for my life. I drove to my buddy's house like I always did before on Sunday mornings.

It was still early and I still continued in prayer about Ohio. As I was parked in front of Dave's house waiting for him, I bowed my head in prayer once again. Sitting behind the wheel of my car with tears now running down my face, I asked the Lord this question: "Lord Jesus do you want me and my family to go to Franklin Ohio to serve in that church. Lord do you want me to go? Is it your will for my life that I go?" When I finished praying I reached over and grabbed my Bible and just opened it at wherever the Lord would direct me to open. As I opened my Bible my eyes were directed to the book of Mark. These are the words that gave me my answer to the direction I was seeking from the Lord. Mark 10:52 "And Jesus said unto him, Go..." These were the first six words that my eyes fell to as I opened my Bible. Those six words were on one line in that verse. They would be a direct answer from God. These six words were a specific answer to my prayers for the past two weeks. They were an incredible answer to my prayer that morning. It was a God and me time that I will cherish for eternity. Here was a direction, a Divine direction, as I found myself at a crossroads in my life. I believe what I experienced was nothing short than a supernatural miracle involving the God of heaven and His Word.

It was wonderful to have met with the Lord of glory in my car that Sunday morning at 8:00am. You talk about tears of joy and heart filled with thanksgiving to the Lord. I was praising Him for blessing me like He did. I couldn't wait to get home that day to tell my wife and son's what happened and how God answered our prayers. I would not see them until church was over since I was serving in the bus ministry as a bus captain. We would attend church together on Sunday evenings. This Sunday evening was going to be an exciting night knowing that Franklin was next on the journey for the Ricci family. So Ohio here we come.

When I got home from church that morning I couldn't wait to tell my family how the Lord gave us direction from His Word to go to Ohio. After we enjoyed lunch together we stayed gathered around the table for awhile because I told them I had some very important news to share about God's Will for us. I noticed everybody was smiling as I began to tell them about meeting with the Lord in my car that morning. When I came to the part about moving to Ohio they all smiled again and said they had peace about moving there even before I got home. Wow, isn't the Lord awesome that He would impress upon the hearts of my family confirmation concerning our new journey. My wife and three son's all said to me, when I finished our family meeting, that they knew in their hearts that we were going to move to Ohio. What a Mighty God we serve! Amen! As I was looking around at my family gathered around our kitchen table I could not help but notice the peace and joy on their faces that only comes from the Lord. We were about to begin a new adventure.

I served as the Associate/Youth Pastor for three years at our church in Ohio. The Lord really blessed our youth ministry there. When we started we had about fifteen or so, but when we left our teen ministry grew to sometimes over fifty. While I was on a mission's trip in Mexico with our teen group the Lord began to move in my heart about pastoring. I was now at the age of 44 and in great spiritual and physical shape. One early morning in April of 1999 I awoke at 4:30 am. I was wide awake and sensing the need to be on my knees and on my face before the Lord. After spending much time in prayer in my living room, I reached for my Bible that was on the coffee table. I turned on the living room light and began to read at the place where I had left off the day before in my quiet time devotions with God. I was reading in the book of Ezekiel in the 12th chapter. This is what the Lord gave me as I began reading verse 3: "Therefore, thou son of man, prepare thee stuff for removing, and remove by day in their sight; and thou shalt remove from thy place to another place in their sight..." As I was meditating on the verses I just read the peace of God flooded my soul and I knew God was going to move us to a different place to serve, but this time He would call me to pastor a church not too far away. It was now about 5:30 am and I just had to go and wake up my wife to show her what the Lord just gave me in my devotional time with Him. Can you imagine what was going on in my wife's mind when at 5:30 in the morning when you are woken up by your husband and are told: "Honey, God is going to move us. I'm going to pastor a church somewhere not too far from here. But I don't know where it is yet." She was very puzzled and soon very excited at the same time waking up to that news. I read her the verses that the Lord had given me earlier from Ezekiel 12. I told her I didn't know where or when but we are going to trust in the Lord and His Word about His plan for our lives.

The following day I called Brother Charles Shafer, one of my Bible professors at Bible College that God had used greatly in my life. I shared with him what the Lord was doing in my life concerning the desire to pastor and the devotion that I had with Lord from Ezekiel 12. He informed me that he had just received a call from a church in Virginia in need of a pastor. This church's pastor had gone home to be with the Lord. I gathered all the information I needed and contacted the church. They requested a resume so I sent them one and our family began to pray again about God's help in our lives. Now the waiting begins. Where are we headed? When will we be leaving for our new ministry? Didn't God show me in His Word we wouldn't be going too far away? Now I have to prepare informing our church about our departure which would not be easy. The Wednesday night that I did break the news to our church was very moving. It was very emotional for all of us. Many tears were shed especially by our teenagers in our youth group. I had just assumed that Virginia is where we would be moving to. Our pastor was very gracious in letting me stay serving there until the time came for us to go.

A few weeks later our church had a missionary family coming to present their ministry to the Indian tribes of New Mexico. I knew them from Bible College in Florida. While Ray and I were talking I shared with him what the Lord was doing in my life. This next part is an amazing "God Thing!" Without me telling him about what I had read from the Bible, he had shared with me that the Lord had given him a few scriptures several nights ago. As he opened his Bible, are you ready for this, he turned to the book of Ezekiel the 12th chapter. He read to me the very same Word of God in verses 1 through 4 that the Lord had given to me just a few days earlier. I was absolutely speechless. No words could describe what was going on in my heart at that moment. I was in awe again of the mighty works of my Lord. How amazing it was to realize how the God of heaven and earth not only spoke to me using theses verse but that He had spoken to another one of His servants to confirm His good, acceptable and perfect will for my life with the same exact portion of scriptures. This was truly a miracle. What are the chances of that happening? There is no way that this just happened by chance. No, this happened by a loving God who desires to bless our lives with clear direction and purpose. You may say that this is unbelievable. I'm living proof that God is concerned about every aspect of your life, especially when you are at a crossroads looking for the right direction to take on your lives journey. The Lord will sometimes lead godly people in your life that will cross paths with you for the purpose of confirming His will if you had any doubts.

It wasn't long that I had received information on a few other churches that were in need of a pastor. There were churches in Georgia, Tennessee, Illinois and even my Bible College that now could be a possibility. Although I was honored to be considered for a position as Singles Pastor at our former church in Florida, I knew the Lord was calling me to pastor a church and not be another associate pastor. So now with the church in Virginia I was looking at five ministry opportunities. How would I know which one? The church in Virginia was supposed to get back in touch with me about arranging a weekend when my family and I could go to visit. In fact I was told that it would most likely be Memorial Day weekend. I would also be going there to preach both Sunday services and pray about the church. While I was still waiting to hear from them I received a call one Sunday after our morning service from a church in Germantown Ohio. This church was in need of someone to fill the pulpit and asked me if I would be willing to preach for them that evening. I got permission from my pastor to go and so I was busy after lunch praying and preparing a message to preach.

This was Sunday May 28, 1999. The day after my wife and I had celebrated 21 years of marriage. I had already prepared a message I was planning to preach at the church in Virginia, so I looked that over for awhile and prayed about preaching from Mark 2:1-12. This message was about four men who carried and then lowered their crippled friend through a hole in the roof that they made, to get him to Jesus. Jesus was this man's only hope to be healed. Their faith in the Son of God was rewarded with their crippled friend having his sins forgiven and his palsy healed. He was blessed both physically and spiritually by the Lord Jesus Christ. This seemed to be the message that the Lord wanted me to bring to the people at this church which was about eight miles away. My family and I were excited about driving only a short distance to the First Baptist Church of Germantown Ohio that Sunday evening. It's funny that I never did get a call from the church in Virginia to confirm my visit with them on this same Sunday. I later found out that the two men that were going to call me to have me at their church thought the other one would have called me. They never did call because it was an oversight on their part. Or was it? Did God somehow allow this mishap to happen so I would be available to preach to a hurting little church in Germantown? Was this another "God Thing" happening in my life?

When my family and I arrived at the church we noticed that there weren't many people there. They seemed to be very friendly and very glad to see us. The church itself was beautiful on the inside with a light colored natural wood setting with burgundy carpet. Now the parking lot was a different story. It needed to be completely resurfaced. The song leader led the small congregation in several songs and after a few church announcements I was introduced as their special speaker for the night. I had great peace and liberty when I preached my message from Mark 2:1-12 about bringing people to Jesus. I gave a closing invitation for anyone desiring to trust Jesus as their Lord and Savior and for those who just wanted to come to the altar a pray. The response of the people was very favorable and even

41

though no one was saved that night I was still encouraged. I did not know until that night that this church was in need of a pastor since their former pastor had resigned in the middle of April. Our family stayed for a short time after the service to fellowship with some of the people there before we made our way back home.

The next day was Monday May 29, 1999. I was up early that morning spending time on my knees in prayer and soon to begin my quiet time of Bible study with the Lord. A time to "Be still, and know that I am God..." like Psalm 46:10 instructs us to. I was in the book of Haggai starting a new chapter that day, it was chapter 2. I began reading with amazement as I sensed the presence of God there with me again. As I got to verse 9 I stopped and went back and read the first 9 verses again. I read them over and over again in awe of what I was seeing. I believe I read these verses at least 7 times when I realized what God was doing in my life. He was giving me His direction and His purpose in my life once again. When I got to verse 3 again I knew in my heart that the Lord was describing to me the First Baptist Church of Germantown Ohio. Although these verses were literally talking about the larger temple of Solomon compared to the smaller temple of Zerubbabel, I knew in my heart God was directing me to First Baptist. Haggai 2:3 "Who is left among you that saw this house in her first glory? And how do ye see it now? Is it not in your eyes in comparison of it as nothing?" Wow, what a description that was so fitting for this church. The church in its early days was a booming church with a large attendance and 13 buses bringing in about 200-300 children alone. It was started on Palm Sunday April 2, 1950 in a downtown storefront on Plum Street by Pastor Cecil Ingram. Now some 49 years later God was calling me to pastor this once great church.

But through the years the church had its rough times which included a lawsuit in 1990 from the former second pastor which made history as recorded in the Bible College textbook: Church, Law and taxes. That was not a good way to make church history. What a nightmare that was. The lawsuit was finally settled and it cost the church dearly in many respects. In fact when our oldest son Jason was attending Bible College in Florida he called me one afternoon to tell me that his teacher just went over our churches lawsuit in class that day. The devil enjoys not only divided churches to destroy them but he longs to divide and destroy homes as well. (Mark 3:25 "And if a house be divided against itself, that house can not stand.") There is nothing like a sweet spirit of unity in a church and in a home. One of the things that are mentioned in the Bible that God actually hates are those sowing discord among His people. In the list of "things doth the Lord hate" found in the Bible, Proverbs 6:19 says "...and he that soweth discord among brethren."

Also in Haggai 2 the Lord mentioned about His glory and His peace in the later house would be greater than the former. And the word "work" also in that portion of scripture was tugging at my heart. Was God describing to me this church and that this is where He was going to direct me to work? Time will tell!

After about a week later I received a call from the church in Tennessee asking me to come preach for them and pray about being their pastor. I did go and preach there but I knew in my heart God was directing to First Baptist in Germantown Ohio. I was really standing at a crossroads in my life with not 4 but now 6 roads to consider. My wife and I began to pray that the Lord would show us clearly and close all the roads but one. Soon I got another call from First Baptist in Germantown asking me to preach for them in June which I did on two occasions. They called me again and asked me to fill their pulpit and preach in July one Sunday. I still wasn't approached about being a possibly candidate for the position of senior pastor of the church. At the end of the July I was invited to come to a church in Georgia to preach and to pray about taking that church over from the pastor who was retiring. My wife and our youngest son Justin came along with us again like he did when we went to Tennessee. Our two oldest, Jason and Sean were working summer jobs at the time and stayed home back in Ohio. I really enjoyed our time in Georgia and the Lord really blessed both the morning and the evening services with one person trusting Christ as their Savior in each service. Before we left the pastor there offered me the church and I told him I believed that God was leading me to wait on the church in Ohio. I thanked him for his offer and consideration.

As the three of us were driving back to Ohio we stopped to get a bite to eat and to check in back home. When I called our house in Franklin our son Jason answered and was all excited to tell me that a man from the church in Germantown had called the other night looking for me and wants me to preach there on Sunday August 1. That wasn't all he said, he continued to tell me that not only did they want me to preach there that day but the church would vote that night about calling me to be there pastor. What a MIGHTY GOD we serve! I was to call this man back as soon as possible because August 1st was the following Sunday. Was this the answer to our prayers? Was this what the Lord was telling me in my quiet time with Him as I read over Ezekiel 12? This church was not even ten miles from my home. It was quite a trip back home to Ohio as we were praising God and blessed again beyond measure.

Sunday August 1st came very quickly and the time did come to see how this day would turn out. I preached both the morning and evening services with great liberty and peace from the Lord. We concluded the evening service with prayer and then we had a question and answer session with me and the 51 people present that night. A really funny moment that night that actually was a real ice breaker happened during the question and answer time. I was asked by one of the men in the church (and this is what I thought he said) what I though about fishing. I replied that I love to fish and I love the outdoors too. The people began to chuckle at my reply and the moderator came up to the platform to inform me that the question was: "what do you think about missions not fishing." I replied with a smile and told them that every church needs to have a heart for missions. It's God plan and His will.

Now it was time for the vote. My family and I were moved into the church nursery as the church gathered for a final discussion and the vote. It seemed like an eternity but soon we were informed that I was now the new Senior Pastor of the First Baptist Church of Germantown Ohio located at 79 Farmersville Pike Our family came back into the church to enjoy a spirit of rejoicing among our new church family. The vote was 50 for and 1 against. You know they say there is always one in the bunch. It was obvious that God was true to His Word. He is always true to His Word, you can count on it.

So here I was on Sunday August 1st, 1999 just voted in as the pastor, just filled with the joy of the Lord. In fact it seems like that the month of August is a very good month for me. I started Bible College in August of 1992, I was ordained and we moved to Ohio in August of 1996 and now its 3 years later and I was so blessed to be called to pastor the First Baptist Church on August 1st. How in the world does a New York Italian former catholic end up in Germantown Ohio being the senior pastor of a Baptist Church? In fact it was in August of 1980 when I trusted the Lord Jesus Christ as my Savior at my Aunt Helen's farm house in Falls, Pennsylvania and became born again by God's grace and mercy. There is no doubt in my mind that there is an ancient G.P.S. that heaven has available to direct all of us on our journey in life. God will, if we let Him, point us in the right direction, when we find ourselves at the crossroads of life.

Chapter Three

"LOOKING AHEAD"

A nother title I had in mind for this book was: "Life's Major Intersections." Sounds like a good subtitle to me. Another thought on a title was: "Finding Direction on Life's Major Intersections." I think most of the time we can agree that there are usually four directions to choose from when we are at an intersection. I have seen a few five way intersections here in this part of Ohio, especially in Germantown where I pastor. On a normal four way intersection it's obvious that we have four choices we can make. We can go either to the right or to the left, turn around and go back or we can go straight ahead. We all notice that there are signs that mark the way for us most of the time. Most of the time they are there but often times we seem to be distracted or just plain not paying attention to the road signs when we are traveling. They are there to direct us to our destination. One of the funniest things I've seen about a road sign was on the internet. It was about a lady who called in to a radio show to suggest that the Deer Crossing signs be moved to areas where the deer would not be encouraged to cross the road or the highway at a dangerous place. She actually thought the deer themselves were directed by those signs to cross in that area. She did not realize that the sign was there to warn the drivers of an approaching deer crossing area and to be cautious driving through that area. It was really funny.

There are times in my journey on this road of life that I was looking for a road sign from God. I prayed and asked the Lord for a sign to confirm that First Baptist Church of Germantown was where he wanted me to go even after I had read my devotional reading from the Bible that morning in Haggai. We like to call this kind of a road sign from God, "putting out the fleece "before the Lord. We find this practice in the Old Testament book of Judges. In chapter 6, (I encourage you to read the entire chapter) we find a man by the name of Gideon who God had called to help the nation of Israel from the threat of their enemies, the Midianites. Gideon was a humble man and was quite overwhelmed with what he was facing. Judges 6:16 "And the Lord said unto him, Surely I will be with thee, and thou shalt smite the Midianites as one man." Gideon's response to the Lord in the next verse, verse 17, is that he needed for the Lord to show him a sign to confirm that it was the Lord talking to him. In verse 21 we see the Lord had consumed the offering by "fire out of the rock" that was under the oak tree. Now you would think that sign from God was enough to convince Gideon, but it wasn't. Gideon was in need of another sign from God that it was God's will and God's direction for him to battle for his life and for Israel's. Gideon needed more assurance of the way he would go so he says to the Lord in verses 36 and 37: "…If thou wilt save Israel by mine hand, as thou hast said, behold, I will put a fleece of wool in the floor; and if the dew be on the fleece only, and it be dry upon all the earth beside, then shall I know that thou wilt save Israel by mine hand, as thou hast said." Well the next morning Gideon sees the ground is dry and he checks the fleece. Sure enough it was exactly as he asked. He was able to wring "the dew out of the fleece, a bowl full of water."

Now you would think that this sign from God was good enough but it wasn't. Gideon decides that he needs to put the fleece out again before the Lord. He was seeking another sign from God to confirm once again God's will for his life. Gideon pleaded with the Lord not to be angry with him in asking Him one more time for a sign. This time Gideon is going to put the fleece out again and ask for a different sign. Judges 6:39 "... with the fleece; let it now be dry only upon the fleece, and upon all the ground let there be dew." God then answers again with another miraculous sign for Gideon. Judges 6:40 "And God did so that night: for it was dry upon the fleece only, and there was dew on all the ground." What was Gideon's problem? Why did he doubt the God of heaven so much? The reason why he was so insecure about this great task is because Gideon was not qualified for such a great task as leading a battle against the enemies of Israel. I once read a great statement that said: "God doesn't called the qualified, He qualifies the called." Gideon's first response to the Lord reflects his heart. Judges 6:15 "And he said unto him, Oh my Lord, wherewith shall I save Israel? Behold, my family is poor in Manasseh, and I am the least in my father's house." Now that's all the Lord needed hear and see from Gideon because that's the kind of heart that God searches for. That's the kind of people that God calls. Remember where God directs you He will protect you. Where the Lord guides you He will provide for you. God will never let you down!

Who am I that I should be critical of Gideon putting out the fleece before God. Why shouldn't he desire a confirmation for such a great military task? Even better reason for me not to judge him is because I practiced "putting out the fleece" myself. As soon as I had my quiet time with God that Monday morning after I preached at First Baptist Church that previous Sunday night, I put the fleece out. I needed a confirmation about whether me being the next pastor of that church was God's will and purpose for my life. I was almost certain the Lord was directing me in that direction but I needed more confirmation. I put the fleeces out before the Lord like Gideon did. No I didn't use my beach towel and asked the Lord to have my towel wet and the sand dry and visa a versa. I just simply met with the Lord on my knees in prayer and asked Him: "Lord

49

Jesus if this is your will for my life and my family about me pastoring this church would you please have someone from the church call for me to candidate on Sunday August 1st. I prayed that prayer on Monday May 30, 1999 and put the fleece out before the Lord. The second fleece was that the night the church would vote to call me as their pastor that it would be by ninety percent or better. That day when my son Jason told me over the phone that someone called from First Baptist requesting that I call them back concerning me candidating for the office of pastor on Sunday August 1st, I was blessed beyond measure. The church wanted me to come that Sunday and preach both services and teach Sunday school as well. After the evening service the church would vote on me to be their pastor. Wow, what a Mighty God we serve! There's one fleece answered and we've got one more to go. That Sunday came and I was as excited as was my wife and sons were waiting to see how the Lord would answer our prayers. The church vote finally came that night and there was only 1 who voted no and 50 who voted yes like I shared in the earlier chapter. I almost received a 100% and so it was that night on August 1st, 1999 that I became the senior pastor of the First Baptist Church of Germantown, Ohio. God is awesome!

As you and I travel on this road of life looking ahead for directions for our future, God will always direct us by His Word, the Bible. Our Divine Mapmaker is one you can put your trust and confidence in. God's promises are found in His Word and they will not only bless you with direction but will also bless you with His peace and safety as you go. There are times that God will also use circumstances as well to confirm His will for your life. There are "signs" from God to look for on your journey especially when you find yourself stuck at a crossroad in your life.

Some of my favorite movies I enjoy watching are; "It's a Wonderful Life", "The Ten Commandments", "The Sound of Music"," Grace Card", "The Secret Life of Jonathan Sperry", "Flywheel", "Facing the Giants" , "Fireproof" and

"Courageous". Kirk Cameron's "Monumental" is a must for every family to see.

There is also a movie that I believe has a powerful message that deals with finding yourself at a crossroads in your life and that movie is "Cast Away." If you haven't seen it yet you need to. In fact just this week they are offering it on Blu-Ray. I'm sure your local library has it for you to check out. I have a DVD player that I got as a Christmas gift one year that filters out all the junk we don't need to hear or see to make a movie worth watching. I think we all really enjoy seeing good, clean family movies like "Finding Nemo", "Happy Feet" or "The Incredibles."

In the movie "Castaway", the opening scene pictures a FedEx truck driving down a country road. When the truck gets to the crossroads it makes a right hand turn at the intersection. The driver comes to a home where there is a young lady who is listening to an Elvis Presley song and welding some artistic angel wings. Her property has some huge awesome angel wings that were set up on her land. On the FedEx package that she ships out there are seen golden angel wings as well, most likely her logo for what she does. Now we fast forward to a FedEx employee, Chuck Nolan (Tom Hanks), who is overseeing a FedEx operation at an European country. In his travels Chuck is able to fly with the FedEx planes using a flight privilege called jump seat. After saying goodbye to the love of his life, he heads to the plane only to turn back to hand her a small gift wrapped box. He purposely did not give this box to her while they were exchanging Christmas gifts in the car before he got out to head to the plane. He tells her not to open it until he comes back from his overseas work assignment. I guess we can assume it was an engagement ring and a wedding would be planned when he returned, so he thought. He tells her: "I'll be right back." Soon he boards the FedEx plane and is flying with a few more FedEx employees, some being pilots.

The plane never reaches its planned destination. The plane runs into some major trouble as it gets caught in a terrible storm, just like we do at times in our life's journey. There are storms heading our way in life that we can avoid if we would only follow the Lord's directions and warnings in His Word. The FedEx plane goes down in the sea and the only one to survive the plane crash is Chuck. The year I believe was 1995 when he finds himself all alone stranded on a small tropical island. After sometime he gets to the point where his life seemed hopeless and was considering suicide. He was thinking he had nothing and no one to live for. He was thinking he had no purpose in life anymore so why not end it. Suicide is never the solution to our temporary problems that God will help us with if we let Him. The devil is the one that drives people to end their life. He is the prince of darkness and despair. He deceives and comes to destroy lives. Satan is a thief who comes to steal your joy. Jesus said in John 10:10 "The thief cometh not, but for to steal, and to kill, and to destroy: I am come that they might have life, and that they might have it more abundantly."

While Chuck is there on that island he finds a small cave for shelter. At one point he begins to draw angel wings on the cave walls. Where did he get the idea to start drawing those wings? Well if you've seen the movie you would remember that some of the planes cargo, which was FedEx packages, washed up on the shore of the small island. Among the packages that he found was a FedEx box that had a set of golden angel wings on it that he would never open. He did open all the other packages that washed up on shore and was able to use much of their contents for survival.

Finally after 4 years on that island he was rescued by a large cargo ship passing by him as he was floating on his man made raft. One of objects he found that washed ashore from the plane wreckage he ended up using as a makeshift sail for his raft. On that makeshift sail he just happened to draw a pair of large golden angel wings. Those angel wings on that FedEx box that he found had made such an impact in his heart and soul. That's what God wants to do in your heart and soul, impact it for all eternity, if you let Him. After the news of Chucks rescue there was a huge welcome home party for him by FedEx. But now after being missing for 4 years he returns to discover that they had a funeral for him using an empty casket. His friends and associates honored his memory by placing some of his favorite things he enjoyed in the casket as they "buried him." The heartbreaker of the story comes when he finds out that the love of his life, Kelly, is now married with children. He expresses his deep regret for leaving her at Christmas. Have you any regrets in your life? We probably all do, but remember, learn from your past and know that God will bless your present life and your future, if you let Him. They soon have a very emotional reunion in which he was able to get his car back that she had parked in her garage and was using herself. He tells her that he should've never have gotten out of the car that night 4 years ago, that he should've never had gotten on that plane.

Oh if we could only turn back the hands of time. If we could only do somethings over and things differently in our lives. As Chuck was looking back and now looking around where he was in his life, it was time for him to look ahead to his future life. What in the world is he going to do now? While Chuck is with one of his co-workers contemplating what to do with his life, he makes this statement:" I know what I have to do now. Tomorrow the sun will rise. Who knows what the tide may bring." I'll shout it from the roof tops, I KNOW WHO KNOWS! GOD KNOWS!! The verses that come to my mind are Jeremiah 29:11-13 "For I know the thoughts that I have toward you, saith the LORD, thoughts of peace, and not of evil, to give you an expected end. Then shall ye call upon me, and ye shall go and pray unto me, and I will hearken unto you. And ye shall seek me, and find me, when ye shall search for me with all your heart." What the tide did bring in to him on that small island was a FedEx box that had some golden angel wings on it. This box he protected and he would not open. He even secured this box on his homemade raft and it weathered the rough storms of the sea with him. Those angel wings from heaven that he claimed saved his life would soon bring him much hope and "an expected end."

The day comes when Chuck decides to drive out to personally deliver this angel winged box to its rightful owner. He finds the house out in the middle of nowhere which just happens to belong to the young lady we see in the opening scenes welding in her barn. The entrance gate is seen to have just her name on it now. No longer does it bear the name of her unfaithful ex husband. Chuck goes to the door to deliver the box only to find no one home. He leaves the box at the door with a note signed by him which reads: "This package saved my life, thank you." He drives back the same way he came and finds himself on the side of the dirt road near the intersection. He gets out a map (no GPS's back then) and tries to figure out what to do now with his life. Where should he go?

Maybe that's where you find yourself right now in your life, looking for direction.

Soon there is someone in a red pickup truck that turns onto the road he just came from to offer him some help. A nice young lady comes out of the truck and says to him, "You look lost and where are ya headed?" He replies that he was just going try to figure that out. She then proceeds to tell him where each of the four ways at the crossroads will take him. She then gets back into her truck and drives away onto the road that Chuck just came from. As she is slowly driving down her road, Chuck notices a set of golden angel wings on the tailgate of her pickup. Here is one my favorite endings to a movie where we see Chuck Nolan now walking out to the middle of the crossroads. Here he is literally at the crossroads of life trying to decide where he should go and what direction to take. What will he do with his life now? Was he still a castaway? It seemed hopeless for a while when he was stranded on that remote island. Then there was the rescue after the raging storms at sea. Soon it seemed even more hopeless after he was rescued realizing what he lost while he was stranded. His wife to be was now married with children, that was devastating. His life seemed to be at a dead end. What will he do, where would he go?

Chuck walks out to the middle of the crossroads, his crossroads, and looks carefully at each direction. He ends up turning and looking ahead to the direction where that nice young lady just drove onto heading to her home. This nice young lady with the golden angel wings on her pickup truck's tailgate to me was his "guardian angel." Soon you see on his face a smile which indicated satisfaction and hope. There was hope in his eyes and a smile on his face because life would go on. That is how we see the movie "Castaway" end, with a new beginning and new hope. We assume he gets into his car to drive back to her house. Assuming he gets to share his heart with this young lady, develop a relationship, soon fall in love and marry. At least that is how I believe the ending should be, a new beginning that was found by looking ahead at the crossroads of life. If you go on your computer and Google: "Scenes from the movie Castaway, stuck at the crossroads" you will view the final scene of the movie. It was pretty cool to see the title of the final scene even after I had chosen the title for this book.

Those golden angel wings gave him hope. That box weathered the storms with him and saved his life. That box gave him promise and strength to go on. Those angel wings led him to his new life and probably to his future wife. I know in my heart that the Lord will help us on our journey. Jesus will help us through the storms of life if we let Him. God will give us the right directions to follow and those directions are found in His Holy Word, The Bible. It's not a magical book, it's a supernatural book. It's a perfect book. It's a pure book. It's a protected book. It's a preserved book. It's a strengthening book. It's a correcting book. It's a guiding book. It's an encouraging book that has weathered the storms of the ages that will direct your life to find purpose and meaning. The Bible is not a good luck book it is a God inspired book. The Bible is God's

Word, His love letter to us. The Holy Bible is our road map to blessings and success.

There is only one place in the entire Bible where we can find the word "success" in the Old Testament book of Joshua. After the death of Moses, Joshua was chosen by God to be the new leader of the children of Israel. Joshua had a great responsibility in leading this extremely large group of people to the Promise Land. The Promise Land was God's will for them and their future. Moses was not able to complete the task or enter the Promise Land himself because he disobeyed God. It was bad enough that Moses' anger caused him to throw down and break the tablets of stone on which God had wrote the Ten Commandments. This happened when he came down off the mountain and seen the people dancing around worshipping a golden calf. God had told Moses that this was going on even before he got down to see it and hear it for himself. I always wondered why Moses didn't just lay those tablets down on the ground first before he confronted that very disturbing situation. Anger got the best of him and brought out his worse like it did when he was told by God to speak to the rock in order to satisfy a thirsty and complaining people. Instead Moses struck the rock in anger and disobeyed God which resulted in him not going into the Promise Land. God did let him see it from a mountain top but He would not let Moses enter in.

A great lesson for all of us to learn is that we must be obedient to the Lord and trust Him regardless of the circumstances around us. We are told in the New Testament book of Ephesians chapter 4 verse 26: 'Be ye angry, and sin not..." I am sure you are familiar with this saying "two wrongs don't make it right." It never has and never will. In Moses' case he really messed up when he rebelled against God's Word. The book of Numbers chapter 20 is where you will find the entire account of the sin of Moses. God gave him clear directions on what to do in Numbers 20:8 "...speak ye unto the rock before their eyes, and it shall give forth water..." What does Moses do after he calls the crowd "rebels" (he should talk) he rebels against the

Word of God and "smote the rock twice… (with his rod) and the water came out abundantly." We need to remember that there are consequences to suffer when we disobey the Lord and His Word. In Moses and his brother Aaron's case neither one would enter into the Promise Land so that's when Joshua is now chosen to lead the people of God after the death of Moses. In the first chapter of the book of Joshua we find the commission of God to Joshua. In Joshua 1:8 we find the only place in the entire Bible where we can find the word "**success**." God tells Joshua : "This book of the law (God's Word) shall not depart out of thy mouth, but thou shalt meditate therein day and night, that thou mayest observe to do according to all that is written therein; for then thou shalt make thy way prosperous, and then thou shalt have good **success**." Did you get that? Meditating on the Word of God day and night, observing to obey His directions will bring good success. Trusting and obeying His Word to find a prosperous way of life.

For Moses, he did not succeed in leading the people of God to the Promise Land. His sin of anger, uncontrolled anger, led him to the sin of rebellion to God's Word. 1 Samuel 15:23 says: "For rebellion is as the sin of witchcraft…" That's pretty serious in the eyes of God. When I read the book of Exodus I think about the warning signs that were in the life of Moses. Exodus 32:16 "And the tables were the work of God, and the writing was the writing of God, graven upon the tables." Those Ten Commandments written on the tablets of stone were the work of God Almighty. What was Moses thinking when he threw them to the ground? I can remember times in my life and ministry that I was guilty of the same thing. I like to refer to it as my Italian temper flaring up. God calls it sin! It is our fallen sin nature, our flesh, which needs to be transformed by the power of God. There were a few times that I messed up what God had done or was doing because of my sinful anger. Oh how I wish I could do somethings over again and handle the problems in a different way. There were times that I would be so furious at some people that I wish I could've just made a phone call and make them disappear. I think you know what I'm talking about. I had the "family connections."

When we are under God's control, under His influence by being filled with the Holy Spirit, we can respond to problems and problem people in a way that is pleasing to the Lord. Galatians 5:16 "This I say then, Walk in the Spirit, and ye shall not fulfill the lust of the flesh." We can respond with compassion by the Holy Spirit or react with anger by the flesh. This is a day by day task for us to accomplish with God's help. That's why it is so needful for us to spend some good uninterrupted quiet time in prayer with God each day and night and reading the Bible.

The S.P.E.C.S. rule is what I enjoy using when I am reading and meditating on the Word of God. If you take this approach in reading your Bible it becomes the most exciting part of your day. It already is the most important part of your day, hearing from God and praising Him through prayer. One should never have an attitude that it's an obligation to read the Bible or pray. It is a privilege to have fellowship with the God of heaven each day. It is a God given honor to enjoy having God's Word available for us to live our lives by with His blessings. It's not about "having to" read our Bible, it's about "needing to" read our Bible. Psalm 119:105 "Thy word is a lamp unto my feet, and a light unto my path." God will show you the way by His wonderful Word if you let him.

You're probably wondering whatever happened to me explaining the S.P.E.C.S. rule to you. Well here it is, when I am in a quiet place praying and reading my Bible I am looking to the Lord to guide my life by using these rules: Sins to confess, Promises to claim, Examples to follow, Commandments to obey and Stumbling blocks to avoid. That's the **S.P.E.C.S. rule.** Here is a great example of this rule that God really used one year while I was attending Bible College that I had already shared with you earlier in the book. I was reading my devotions on the morning that I had to make a decision about whether or not to take out that $5,500.00 Stafford loan offered to me. As I continued to read an extra chapter in the book of Deuteronomy, chapter 15, there was an obvious answer to my prayer and a "command to obey" for me in neon lights (well not literally but spiritually). In verses 5 and 6 God made it very clear what I was not to do that day by His command which was: "Thou shalt not borrow…" Isn't that AMAZING! God gave me a "command to obey" that answered a specific prayer request of mine concerning a financial decision.

There are many Bible reading plans available to follow. The most common is just starting in the book of Genesis and reading at least 1 or 2 chapters a day. Another system is to read a few chapters from the Old and New Testament each day. I like to recommend starting in the New Testament with the book of Matthew. Read 1 or 2 chapters a day until you have read through the entire New Testament. There are so many people who have never read through the Bible, even the New Testament. I would also like to recommend reading a chapter out of the book of Proverbs each day of the month that corresponds to the actually day. Proverbs contains 31 chapters so this works really well when there are months that have 31 days. So on the first day of the month you read Proverbs chapter 1 and on the second day of the month you read Proverbs chapter 2 and so on. When you have a month that has less than 31 days just read those extra chapters on that day or night. Some of my favorite passages in the book of Proverbs are found in Proverbs 3:5, 6 "Trust in the Lord with all thine heart, and lean not unto thine own understanding. In all thy ways acknowledge him, and he will direct thy paths." Oh yes He will direct you as you look ahead, but only if you let Him! The book of Proverbs is the book of wisdom and how we all need God's wisdom to help direct our lives each and everyday.

Another great place to read in the Bible for some awesome quiet time with God is in the book of Psalms. One of my favorite passages and most often quoted is Psalm 23 which begins with: "The Lord is my shepherd, I shall not want." That verse is telling me that there is a very satisfied life to those who follow the Lord. Read Psalm 23 for yourself and discover the ways God desires to bless your life if you let Him. What I see in this Psalm is not only a very satisfied life with my relationship with God but assurance that He will supply for His sheep. He supplies rest, guidance, protection, restoration and refreshment for my soul. My Shepherd also blesses me with His presence, His comfort, His anointing and best of all His eternal security. Let me encourage you with this thought when you read Psalm 23 and when you reach verse 6 which says: "Surely goodness and mercy shall follow me all the days of my life, and I will dwell in the house of the Lord forever." So here is an awesome truth to ponder as we follow the Lord, hear His voice and obey His Word. The blessings of God are following us as we follow the Lord. The goodness of God and the mercy of God are following you to bless your life with all that He promises us in His Word. But once we make a choice and decide not to follow the Lord and go our own way, we can not expect the goodness of God and the mercy of God to follow us. They won't. They are only behind us, following us, if we are following the Lord and his Word. The blessings of God on our lives are the results of our obedience to Him, His Word, His Will and His Way. They go with me only on that condition.

We must be on guard to avoid getting distracted and detoured from following our Lord Jesus. The devil will try to deceive you and the things of this world will try to detour you off the path that God has for you. When that happens, and it will, remember that God will try to guide you back to the place where He wants you to be by the Holy Spirit and His Word. I love this passage in Isaiah 30:21 which says: "And thine ears shall hear a voice behind thee, saying, this is the way, walk ye in it, when ye turn to the right hand, and when ye turn to the left." It's not an audible voice that you hear but "a still small voice" of God that will lovingly guide you in your heart by His Holy Spirit and His Word.

Here are a few words of caution from the Bible. The first I'll share with you is Proverbs 16:25 "There is a way that seemeth right to a man, but the end thereof are the ways of death." This is the way that leads to "the dead end" of life which needs to be avoided. It all comes down to what you do and how respond to the Word of God. The choice is simple: our way or God's Way. There is a pretty clear warning that we find in Deuteronomy 11:26-28 "Behold, I set before you this day a blessing and a curse: A blessing, if ye obey the commandments of the LORD your God, which I command you this day: And a curse, if ye will not obey the commandments of the LORD your God, but turn aside out of the way which I command you this day..." The LORD has wonderful blessings and promises for us to enjoy but we must meet the conditions which in most cases are just simply trusting God in obedience to His Word. Did you notice the two letter word "if" here in this portion of scripture? All throughout the Bible, Old and New Testaments, you will discover the promises of God that will include the words "if" and "then." These spell out the conditions to follow or the commandments to obey in order to enjoy the blessings of God's promises.

There is a false teaching among "Christian" churches today that promotes a "name it and claim it" super faith religion. So many good hearted people have been deceived by these false teachings. We have no right or power "to speak "anything to anyone including ourselves, especially when it does not line up with the Word of God.

Remember what God promises in Joshua 1:8, a prosperous and successful life God's way. In order for you to enjoy that blessing we are told to spend time in God's Word day and night doing all that He directs you to do. Joshua 1:8 makes it very clear when the LORD says: "...for **then** thou shalt make thy way prosperous, and **then** thou shalt have good success." Notice the Bible says that you will make your way prosperous and successful when you "observe to do according to all that is written therein..." We have Divine directions to follow in God's Powerful Scriptures in order to enjoy the blessings of God. Did you get a chance to read the back cover of this book? Remember my reference to the day when the disciples went fishing all night and caught nothing. It's obvious they were not prosperous or successful after many hours of hard work in their boats. What made the difference that morning? It's really **Who** made the difference! The difference was following the specific directions of the Lord Jesus Christ. The results were an extremely blessed day with a catch of a "multitude of fishes." Wouldn't you agree that the disciples enjoyed a very prosperous and very successful day that was blessed by the Lord Jesus Christ? Their day was ultimately blessed by their obedience to His Word and so will yours be, if you let Him direct your life. I encourage you sometime today or right now if you can to read all of John chapter 21 about the account of Jesus' appearance by the sea. I love it when I hear and read about how people's lives were blessed by Jesus.

It's funny how I have a womans "voice" in front of me now for the past few years giving me directions to my desired destination, my G.P.S. unit. I've had a G.P.R. "unit" sitting next to me giving me directions and driving instructions way before I had a G.P.S. unit. I am referring to my precious wife Gayla, her initials are: G.P.R. You know what I mean! Don't you just love it when you hear that "voice" from your G.P.S. unit say "recalculating" when you're traveling the wrong way? It will attempt to redirect you in order for you to reach your destination. God will do the same thing by His Word and the Holy Spirit. These little units amaze me and are very helpful when we travel. Personal navigation systems were first used by the military as handheld units. Our modern G.P.S. units are supported by about twenty four satellites that orbit the earth. What good is it if we don't follow the directions from our G.P.S. units? Sadly to say that there are many people who have a Bible, attend church regularly, hear a message from the Word of God and fail to follow God's direction for their lives. I believe this satellite communication system was first God's idea anyway.

God's Positioning System was so very clear in the sky one night over two thousand years ago directing some wise men who were searching for a new born king, the Lord Jesus. The Gospel of Matthew gives us the record of heavens GPS, God's Pointing Star that these wise men were following. Matthew 2:1,

2 "Now when Jesus was born in Bethlehem of Judea in the days of Herod the king, behold, there came wise men from the east to Jerusalem, saying, Where is he that is born King of the Jews? For we have seen his star in the east, and are come to worship him." Little did they know they were only about five miles away from finding Jesus. When Herod consulted the chief priest and scribes he demanded they tell him where this new king should be born. They told him in Bethlehem of Judea as the prophet Micah foretold in Micah 5:2 and yet they themselves even though they knew some bible facts were not looking for the Messiah to come. You wonder why they didn't get all excited and request to follow with the wise men to find this newborn King. Herod then sends the wise men to Bethlehem to find the child and bring back word to him as where he maybe found. Herod lies to them when he tells them he wanted to know because he himself desired to go and worship him. We pick up the account in Matthew 2:9-11 "When they had heard the king they departed; and lo, the star, which they saw in the east, went before them, till it came and stood over where the young child was. When they saw the star, they rejoiced with exceeding joy. And when they were come into the house, they saw the young child with Mary his mother, and fell down, and worshipped him: and when they had opened their treasures, they presented unto him gifts; gold, and frankincense, and myrrh."

You see over two thousand years ago it was God who had the first idea of creating and using a G.P.S. to direct these wise men to find His only begotten Son, our Lord Jesus. Think about this, the star led these men to Jerusalem where these wise men stopped and received more information about this King they were searching for. Where did they get this information from? They got it from people who had some knowledge of the Old Testament prophecies of the Messiah which was found in the book of Micah. Then from there the star led them to the exact location, the very house that they were looking for where Jesus was. Isn't that amazing? What a Mighty God we serve. These gifts that were given by the wise men were gifts worthy of a king. Here's a good question to stir your heart, what gifts will you give Jesus this Christmas? What treasure will you open and give to the Lord? How about your time, your talents, your treasures and your testimony for His glory and His honor? On that first Christmas day the angels did declare his birth to the shepherds in the field that night. The angel also told these shepherds where to find Him, "in the city of David" which was Bethlehem. Then the shepherds were given a specific place, an unusual place to find Jesus in Luke 2:12 "And this shall be a sign unto you; you shall find the babe wrapped in swaddling clothes, lying in a manger." Luke 2:16 "And they came with haste, and found Mary, and Joseph, and the babe lying in a manger." Luke 2:20 "And the shepherds returned, glorifying and praising God for all the things that they had heard and seen, as it was told unto them." The angel was a messenger of God with the most incredible birth announcement known to man. The Christmas story never gets old to me. I always shed a tear or two when I preach about the love of God, especially about the true meaning of Christmas. When you really take time to focus on how awesome God is you can't help but see how He desires to bless our lives, if we let Him.

Psalm 119:24 "Thy testimonies also are my delight and my counselors." Clearly we see we are to rely on God's word for counsel. Godly counsel is when God's Word is applied to our hearts and minds by the Holy Spirit of God by godly people. Psalm 119 is a wisdom Psalm that conveys the idea that God's Word contains everything man needs to know. I encourage you to read through this Psalm by reading 8 or 16 verses at a time by following the pattern of how it was structured. Take time to meditate on these words and memorize the verses that will tug at your heart. Try reading them out loud to yourself. I suggest you read each group of 8 verses at least 3 times slowly. Praying as you read, asking the Lord to speak to your heart through His Word. As you read this Psalm you will notice different words that refer to God's Word. The word "law" is used meaning that God will give you instruction. "Testimonies" is what God testifies of

His will. "Judgments" is what God has ruled. "Statues" is what God has given as law. The word "precepts" is what God has ordered and "word" refers to what God has promised or said. By the way, God will never go back on His Word or His promises.

Basically when you are looking for God's direction in your life you need to be sure that God's Word is an agreement. For example, make sure that you are not overlooking or ignoring a Bible principle or a command to obey. God's Word makes it real clear that we should always be honest about everything and never compromise the truth. If we do we damage our integrity. A good name is worth a lot in the eyes of God when we honor Him in all we do and say. Proverbs 22:1 "A good name is rather chosen than great riches..." The next principle to follow will help you determine if God is leading you in a certain area or in a certain direction. This sometimes is made very obvious as the Lord will allow different circumstances to happen in your life while you are seeking His direction and guidance. There is an unsettling in your heart and soul when we began to step out of the path the God has for us. There is a lack of peace of mind when we wander off His Way. There is conviction in your soul when you fight against the Holy Spirit's work in your life. Then there is the peace of God that passes all understanding that guards your heart and mind when you are following the Lord's Way.

When you make choices that please and honor God you will know it. Don't ever settle for less than God's best for your life. There is not only a peace that you will experience but a joy as well when you find and follow His will, His direction and His way for your life. Just do it! It's not always going to be easy. This doesn't mean that you won't be heading into some rough traveling conditions, some bumps in the road. There will be trials you will face but remember this important truth; you will not face them alone because God will be with you. He promised that He would never leave you nor forsake you. That's why it is so important that you "Pray without ceasing" and stay faithful to the Lord and His Word. There are times you may need to spend not only a long season of prayer but a time of fasting as well.

Fasting is a time when you need to skip a meal or two and spend that time in prayer and reading God's Word to help you with your situation. Praying while fasting is powerful. I believe this practice is much ignored today in the life of the child of God. I have personally experienced God answer my prayers especially while I was attending Bible College in a very powerful way. There was no way that me being 37 years old, married with 3 sons and working a part time job could ever do as well as I did in my classes without the Lord's help. Lenard Ravenhill once said that "preaching moves people but prayers affects God.'

I really enjoy what God has called me to do with my life. I feel so blessed and so unworthy at the same time to be privileged to teach and preach God's Holy Word. To be His messenger boy, His bread boy and His servant is such an awesome blessing. I agree with Brother Ravenhill when it comes to praying that moves the heart of God. I have been moved many times by men of God that were filled with the Holy Spirit preaching the Word of God. Truthfully it was God working through these men by His Word to bless my heart. But as much that Spirit filled preachers move us, remember that your prayers, your words, your voice, your tears and your cries move the heart of God.

As you look ahead with great anticipation, know in your heart that the God of heaven can and will direct your life. Here are some facts about the Bible that will help you as you pray and seek His guidance: Jesus Christ is the heart of the Bible. He is the central theme of the Word of God. One of my favorite passages in the gospel of Luke that supports this is found Luke 24:25-27. Jesus was walking on the road to Emmaus soon after He was raised from the dead. He soon joins two of His disciples on the same road who were not able to recognize him because Jesus had disguised himself. Jesus concealed his true identity and made like He didn't know what had transpired the last few days. Jesus then proceeded to share with them probably the most incredible Bible history lesson about Himself that was ever shared. "Then he said unto them, O fools, and slow of heart to believe all that the prophets have spoken: Ought not Christ to have suffered these things, and to enter into his glory? And beginning at Moses and all the prophets, he expounded unto them all the scriptures the things concerning himself." Did you get that? Jesus explains to these two disciples what Moses, who wrote the first five books of the Bible, and what the Old Testament prophets wrote about Him.

The Holy Bible is made up of 66 books. There are 39 books that make up the Old Testament and 27 books that make up the New Testament. The Bible was written by 40 authors that covered a period of about 1600 years. There are 929 chapters in the Old Testament and 260 chapters in the New Testament. That makes a total of 1,189 chapters in the Holy Bible. The longest chapter is Psalm 119 which has 176 verses. The shortest chapter is Psalm 117 which has only 2 verses. The longest verse is in Esther 8:9 and the shortest verse is found in John 11:35, which have only 2 powerful words: "Jesus wept." Now are you ready for the most amazing, heart moving fact about God's Holy Bible? The middle verse, I mean the very center of the Bible is Psalm 118:8 "It is better to trust in the Lord than to put confidence in man." Here we go, hold on tight! Let's do the math. If you would divide Psalm 118:8 in half you would find that you have 6 verses to the left and 6 verses to the right. (Six is the number or symbol for man in the Bible) Looking at the very heart of that verse, the very heart of the Holy Bible, what two words are in the center? You got it, **"the LORD."** Wow, is that not amazing that God would by inspiration move on the hearts of these forty authors to write His Holy Bible and also bless us with this awesome fact of **Who** is the heart of His Book. There are skeptics that may say that just happens to be a coincidence, I don't think so! I say it's a God thing. Think about it, the number 6 is symbolic of man and in between the front 6 verses and the back 6 verses you find **"the LORD."** That is why we need to stand in awe of His Word.

The devil does not want you to spend quiet time reading God's Word. The devil also wants you to forget about praying and worshipping the Lord. Satan would rather you not find

God's direction for your life. He is a master when it comes to deceiving people. Satan's plan is to deceive and ultimately to destroy lives. His name Satan (Matthew 4:10) means "adversary", the enemy of God and man. Other names given to him are: Lucifer, son of the morning (Isaiah 14:12), the devil (Matthew 4:1,5,8 ,11), the wicked one (Matthew 13:19,38), the prince of this world (John 12:31), the god of this world (2 Corinthians 4:4), an angel of light (2 Corinthians 11:4), the prince of the power of the air (Ephesians 2:2), a roaring lion (1 Peter 5:8 "Be sober, be vigilant, because your adversary the devil, as a roaring lion, walketh about, seeking whom he may devour.), the great dragon, that old serpent (Revelation 12:7,9), the accuser of our brethren (Revelation 12:10). Satan was a very powerful angel created by God who rebelled against God and was cast out of heaven, (Isaiah 14:12-20). One third of the angels, who are now demon spirits, were cast out with him. Satan's rank was that of a cherubim (Ezekiel 28:12-14), which was of the highest order of all the angels.

The devil would like nothing more than to deceive you into following a road that leads to disappointment. Satan will lead you to a road that will cause discouragement, darkness and depression in your life. The wicked one has a road that ultimately leads to death. A road that may seem to be the right way but is not. The book of Proverbs has a warning in Proverbs 14:12"There is a way which seemeth right unto a man, but the end thereof are the ways of death." The prince of darkness will tempt you in anyway he can. The devil's most successful way to destroy lives and families is to tempt you to get on "Addiction Alley." Our enemy uses addictions of all kinds to devour lives and to destroy families. Satan wants you on his alley that leads you to the addiction of alcohol, drugs, pornography and gambling. You maybe on one or more Satan's alley's right now. I have four different names for the enemy's roads that will lead you to "Addiction Alley" which is THE DEAD END OF LIFE: Satan's Street, Lucifer's Lane, Devil's Drive and Adversary Avenue.

Satan is a thief and a liar that will use whatever and whoever he can to keep you off the Romans Road of salvation. This Romans Road leads to Heavens Highway. Satan does not want you to find God's will for your life and be blessed. Jesus said in John 10:10 "The thief cometh not, but to steal, and to kill and to destroy: I am come that they might have life, and have it more abundantly." This abundant life is a more superior quality of life that Jesus promises us when we repent of our sins and when we receive Him into our lives as our Lord and Savior. It's a blessed life that only comes by Jesus Christ. Jesus went on to say in John 10:11 "I am the good shepherd: the good shepherd giveth his life for his sheep." Jesus gave His life so you can enjoy everlasting life and a blessed life. You maybe asking yourself right about now: "How do I obtain such a life that God has for me?" I am so glad that you asked that because for the answer to that question we must now look up!

Chapter Four

"LOOKING UP"

———— ❧ ————

P salm 5:1-3 "Give ear to my words, O Lord, consider my meditation. Hearken unto the voice of my cry, my King, and my God: for unto thee will I pray. My voice shalt thou hear in the morning, O Lord: in the morning will I direct my prayer unto thee, and will look up." This Psalm is a prayer of David like most of the Psalms are. David was facing a crisis in his life. I can remember as a child that I would lie awake looking up from my bed on many nights praying to my grandfather, Dominic Ricci, hoping he would hear me from heaven and help me. Our family was in a mess. We were in crisis mode most of the time. Our troubled home life was very hard on me and my two sisters. Even when my father remarried a few years after he divorced my mom, all three of us found ourselves in another crisis situation. We weren't really accepted or welcomed by our new "family." To tell you the truth it was extremely awkward and very uncomfortable to call another woman "mom" when she really wasn't your mom. My heart goes out to mistreated step children, and if you are a step child maybe you know exactly what I am talking about. Step parents can be a blessing or they can be a curse. There are a few good books available by Christian authors about step parenting that will help families with this major life adjustment. I know that my younger sister

Mary and I tried our best to adjust, even at our young ages. I believe I was 12 years old and she was 10 years old at this time.

One of our worst experiences my sister Mary and I had with our step mother was when we were doing the dishes together one night. Our dad left early to go bowling and my sister was washing the dishes while I was drying and putting them away. Our step mother came in the kitchen when we were about finishing up with the dishes. She picked up a dish that my sister had just washed and left for me to dry. I was in the restroom at the time and ready to dry the rest of the stack of dishes when I got back to the kitchen. From our bathroom I heard my father's wife yelling at my sister. It seemed no matter what we did nothing pleased that woman. She made our lives miserable. It wasn't long that my sister was cracked over the head with one of the dishes that she had just washed. My father's wife wasn't happy about finding a few small dish soap bubbles left on the dish after she had inspected from the stack. She yelled and accused my sister of not washing the dishes properly. My sister was devastated and was so upset. It was so sad that my Dad never did see that side of this woman until he was much older. I really don't know remember how this all was resolved or explained to my Dad, but I'm sorry, to me this was abuse. She was like a split personality when she was around us. Funny how she was one way when my dad was home and another way when he wasn't home. Most of the time it felt like we were in a prison in that house with no way out. We especially dreaded Saturday mornings. It was housework day all morning long. Me and the vacuum cleaner would spend most of the morning on Saturdays working together to clean our assigned rooms. Heaven knows what would happen if we had finished "too early" with work. I remember I would be lying on the rug between the beds with the vacuum running just to add more time to the cleaning chores. It seemed the longer we "cleaned" the happier our step mom was. I could remember when I would vacuum my dad's room that I would help myself with some of his lose change. I would usually find some in his closet. After all, I thought a little candy money would be a proper reward for all the hard work I had done. But to be honest with you that was stealing and very sinful. A few years after I became a Christian I confessed to my Dad all of the sinful things I had done including stealing his change. Is there anything you need to confess to someone?

My sister Mary decided to move out after that horrible experience and move in with our real mom in White Plains. That wasn't the greatest place to move to but it was better than being in a home where there was a lack of love and respect. I decided to stay and tough it out. I thought to myself that this lady wasn't about to get her way and run me out of the house too. Every night when I was lying in bed I would look up and pray for help. I would beg God to help me while I would cry and pray through the night. My Dad was not happy with the situation at home either. He had a long talk with her one night and things seem to calm down a little. A few years went by when I finally moved out after I had purchased a small home in Elmsford New York in August of 1977. I had a nice little home and great peace of mind when I moved into that cute little white cape cod home on South Stone Avenue. I lived there alone until I married my wife Gayla in May of 1978.

I would like to share with you one of the darkest times of my life and ministry. It was a day of crisis for me and a sweet couple in my church. It was a time when I looked up and wept like I never wept before. It was a time so dark that my faith in the Lord was shaken. There was a godly young couple in my church expecting their second child. It was a wonderful time in our church when we would announce that a couple was expecting a child, a blessing which was a gift from God. Everything seemed to be fine until one Sunday morning I noticed this couple looking burdened about something. Then at the close of the church service I noticed the young pregnant mother making her way down to altar at the front of the church. She slowly knelt down and bowed her head in prayer. After she finished praying she slowly walked back to her seat. I noticed she was wiping away some tears from her eyes as she was walking up her aisle. My wife came to me after the service and informed me that this pregnant mom was no longer feeling her baby move anymore and she was very distraught with the thought of what the doctors would tell her. She had a doctor's appointment the next day. When that day arrived it wasn't long that she was told that her 5 month old baby in her womb had passed away. The doctor could not detect a heartbeat and gave this godly couple the heartbreaking news. I received a phone call from this heartbroken couple and I rushed over to comfort them. As we prayed together, we wept and held each other for quite some time. They asked me to be with them in the hospital delivery room when they would deliver their baby. I said I would be there for them. I loved this couple. They were the sweetest people you'll ever want to meet.

I began to question God, asking Him why He allowed this to happen to this family. Anger and bitterness began to take root in my heart. The day came when she delivered her baby, he was a boy. They were praying for a son I believe so why did God take him while he was still in the womb? In that room there was an enemy that was very present. This enemy was very dark. This enemy was death. I held this little fully-formed baby boy in my arms who was wrapped in a blanket. Oh how I cried bitterly that day, we all cried. We had a private family funeral where we shed even more tears together during the closed casket service. A beautiful little white casket and the use of the funeral home were donated by the funeral director. Out of the kindness of his heart and the tragedy that we all experienced, he felt led to donate his services to this heartbroken couple. During the funeral service, I noticed him weeping for this family. I shared from II Samuel 12:23, where David said after his child passed away, "But now he is dead, where fore should I fast? Can I bring him back again? I shall go to him, but he shall not return to me." Although I was praying God would bring them comfort that only He could bring, I was really struggling. In my heart I wrestled whether to give up on the ministry.

For a few months I was in a dark place of despair. It was a place that the devil wanted me to be in, a place of darkness, depression, and distress. This was a place that God did not want me to be in. In times like this, we especially need to trust in the Lord, but I was having a really hard time. Finally, several months later, after much prayer and fasting, God gave me peace and healed my bitter spirit. Several years later, this couple was expecting again. When we were told, I prayed with the expecting mom, and begged the Lord to bless her with another son. The day came of her delivery. She made it through to her full term. As I walked through the hallway down to her room, her family was outside waiting to hear the news. As I approached them, they all told me that she had a girl. I was a little disappointed, but God knows best. It seemed that they overheard them referring to "her" when the doors opened and the nurse came out. With that being overheard, all of us assumed it was a baby girl. Finally, after what seemed like an eternity, the proud dad emerged from the delivery room just beaming with joy as he said, "It's a boy!" We were all puzzled and stunned by his statement. And then he had a very puzzled look because of our reaction. And for a few minutes in that hallway, there was a big group of puzzled people wondering what in the world was going on. We told him why we first thought it was a girl, and we all laughed, and began to cry at the same time. God is so good, all the time. The funny thing was when I was told it was a girl at first I called my wife and our church secretary to give them the news of the "baby girl" that was born. Then after the proud father came out to give us the news that it was a baby boy, I had to call them all back to tell them I had made a mistake, and that the baby was a boy. My wife thought maybe I was having a low blood sugar moment, or something, or just joking.

We all go through tough times. Some trials of life are unavoidable. Even when we are on the right road going in the right direction, storms will come. I thought that that was the darkest time in my life that I ever experienced, with the passing of that 5 month-old, premature baby boy. I was wrong. There was another dark time coming my way, but this one would be the most overwhelming and darkest day of my life.

Our church had been praying for the daughter-in-law of one of our faithful members and Sunday School teachers who was hospitalized with liver cancer. The doctors gave her such little hope. We prayed every day for the Lord to heal her, but the cancer was too far spread and soon it would take her. She was a Christian, so her ultimate healing was for her to be absent from the body and to be present with the Lord I received a call on June 17, 2009 of her passing in the hospital. That night I began praying for direction on what to share at her funeral since the services would be held at my church. Death brings so much darkness and sorrow. The next morning, Thursday June 18th, I answered our home phone around 7:30 in the morning; it was my wife's brother, Dean. He was on the phone and sounded very upset, and asked me to put my wife on the phone. I handed my wife the phone. In a few seconds she began to scream and cry as she said, "Mommy is dead? This can't be!" It was a shock, I thought it was a nightmare, a really bad dream, but unfortunately it wasn't. My mother-in-law was such a warm, fun-loving woman. Her family was blessed to have her. Panic set in the heart of my wife. I knew I had to get her to New York as quickly as possible. I couldn't understand how this tragedy happened. Mom wasn't sick, although she had a pacemaker; there were no signs of any health issues. The night before she passed away, she spent time with her daughter, eating her favorite flavor of ice cream: chocolate and peanut butter. That morning, my father-in-law had his youngest daughter call 9-1-1 because he noticed that mom was not breathing. The emergency response team came and did their very best to try to revive her, but they were not successful.

My wife and I had wept as we held each other and prayed for our family. We notified our sons about the passing away of their grandmother, and our oldest son, Jason, was able to fly to New York with my wife that afternoon to be with her family that evening. Sean and his wife, Amanda, and our youngest son, Justin, would come up the next day. The viewing was set for that Sunday, and the funeral service on Monday. Now I was preparing, not only for the funeral on Saturday at our Ohio church, now, I was preparing for the funeral service for my mother-in-law for Monday. The service was to be held at a Catholic church in Sleepy Hollow, where I would be able to share a short message from God's Word in her honor. The graveside service was entirely my responsibility. I made arrangements to fly out after the funeral service at my church in Ohio on Saturday . I asked another pastor who was the uncle of the man who's wife had passed away to do the graveside service. My spirit was overwhelmed, and my heart was very heavy. Grief and sorrow were now flooding my soul.

On that Friday, I was in my church office praying and studying for Saturday's funeral service. I was also looking over some Scriptures I was praying about preaching on Monday in New York at my mother-in-law's graveside service. As I was praying, I sensed the peace and presence of God touch me as I began to weep over the families who had suffered the loss of their loved ones. It was even harder on my wife and I, because we had made prior arrangements to visit our families in New York for the following week. Several years before, the same thing happened when my father passed away in Florida while he was staying in a nursing home. When I finally found out where he was, I made flight arrangements to go visit him. But he got ill, and passed away very quickly, the week before I was to be out there to visit. Now, almost the same thing happened. I was finishing up the order of service for the funeral on Saturday at my church, when my office phone rang. As I answered the phone, one of my church members was in a panic and very desperate as she told me that her brother-in-law just shot himself behind their barn, and they believed that he was dead. They begged me to come over there as quickly as I could. I dropped everything and rushed over there. I don't even remember how fast I was going, because I didn't care. I knew there was a family in great need. I rushed over there as quick as I could to find myself in a place that I had never been before. I wasn't sure how to comfort someone who had lost a loved one by suicide. I was lost for words. How can you pray? What do you pray? Can I pray?

It wasn't long that the Lord put a few comforting verses on my heart that I shared with the hurting family. God's Word and His presence put some relief in a very dark place at a very dark time in that home. This man was a Christian. He was battling depression. He was on heavy medication and having a really bad week. Suicide is never the answer to your problems. After spending some time with the hurting wife and the family, I left to go back to my church. I was talking to God all the way back to the church. I told Him that I could not handle anything else and I was at my breaking point. Death was surrounding me once again. Darkness and despair was creeping into my soul. Satan was now getting an advantage. Three people who died, one right after the other, on three separate days was too much for me to handle. I couldn't handle it. I didn't want to handle it. I came back to the church, walked down the aisle to the auditorium's altar, and threw myself at the mercy of God. I cried and I wept to the Lord, begging Him to help me, that I could not do this without His strength and presence in my life. I can almost picture the devil telling God that I would curse God because of all that happened, especially with my mother-in-law.

In the book of Job we find that's exactly what Satan desired that Job, the servant of God, would do; curse God and die because of all the tragedy in his life. But Job never did curse God, in fact he stayed faithful and God blessed Job with twice as much as he lost. God also blessed Job with more children to replace the ones he lost as well.

My soul was being afflicted by my enemy, Satan. He was troubling my mind; he was troubling my will and my emotions, which makes up my soul. If there was a time in my life that I must look up to the Lord for some help, it was now. King David writes in Psalm 143, "Hear my prayer, O Lord, give ear to my supplications; In thy faithfulness answer me, and in thy righteousness. And enter not into judgment with thy servant; for in thy sight shall no man living be justified. For the enemy hath persecuted my soul, he hath smitten my life down to the ground, he hath made me to dwell in darkness, as those that have been long dead. Therefore is my spirit overwhelmed within me, my heart within me is desolate. I remember the days of old, I meditate on all thy works; I muse on the work of thy hands. I stretch forth my hands unto thee: my soul thirsteth after thee, as a thirsty land. Selah. Hear me speedily, O Lord: my spirit faileth: hide not thy face from me, lest I be like unto them that go down into the pit. Cause me to hear thy loving kindness in the morning; for in thee do I trust: cause me to know the way wherein I should walk; for I lift up my soul unto thee. Deliver me, O Lord, from mine enemies: I flee unto thee to hide me. Teach me to do thy will, for thou art my God: Thy spirit is good; lead me into the land of uprightness. Quicken me, O Lord, for thy name's sake, for thy righteousness sake, bring my soul out of trouble. And of they mercy cut off mine enemies, and destroy all them that afflict my soul, for I am thy servant." Just like David was seeking the Lord to hear him, to lead him, to teach him, to quicken him (which means to make him alive or to revive him), I was in desperate need of this kind of help from the Lord. My life was overwhelmed. Ministry was too heavy for me to handle. I am so thankful that God is faithful to His Word. He did hear my prayer. He did give me strength. He did give me His peace that passes all understanding. One of my favorite verses is found in Jeremiah 33:3. "Call unto me, and I will answer thee, and shew thee great and mighty things, which thou knowest not."

We need to remember that God's comfort and strength will come when you call unto the Lord in prayer and supplication. There are many broken hearts and crushed spirits that God can heal, if only people would turn to Him. Thomas Moore was a singer and poet, whose personal life was overwhelmed with tragedy. He lost all five of his children during his lifetime.

Listen to his words and read this out loud: "Here, bring your wounded hearts, here, tell your anguish: earth has no sorrow that heaven cannot heal." But, you need to look up when you find yourself at that crossroads in life. Psalm 121:1,2 "I will lift up my eyes unto the hills, from whence cometh my help. My help cometh from the Lord, which made heaven and earth." Psalm 123:1 "Unto thee lift I up mine eyes, O thou that dwellest in the heavens."

There are times that God will send people your way to help you on your journey. These are called Divine appointments from above. Have you ever by chance just run into someone and realized sometime later that God must have directed that person to cross your path at the moment that you needed someone there? We refer to them as a "God-send." This is my prayer for you as you continue to read this book, that God will use it to help you in your life's journey. I don't know where you are on that path you're traveling on. Just maybe some light has been shed and some help given to better direct you in your journey. Life is all about choices. The choices we make are not only for that moment, but will most likely have an effect years later. Every day we are faced with choices. Some are very easy to make, while others take time and prayer to decide. Any choice that is in front of you that tempts you to sin against God, realize that temptation is from your enemy, the devil. Sometimes our worst enemy can be the one looking back at you in the mirror. This is especially true when we outright rebel against God's Word and rebel against God's will for our lives.

I'm sure Jonah was not a happy camper spending three days and three nights in the belly of a whale. He had no one to blame but himself after he had rebelled against God's Word and God's will for his life. Jonah had specific directions from God which was to go to Ninevah and preach God's message to the people of that place. He had God's will given to him very clearly but he refused. Jonah, being a rebellious servant of God, caused the others on the ship that he was on to have a rough time on that boat. A terrible storm threatened the life of everyone on that ship. I like to call that ship the S.S. Rebellion. For the life of me, I can't figure out why Jonah took so long to pray to the Lord while he was in the belly of the whale for three days. God heard his prayer and gave Jonah a second chance. God prepared that whale for Jonah's protection from drowning; God prepared that whale for Jonah's punishment for sinning against God. God prepared that whale to get Jonah ready to be submissive to His Word and to His way. Jonah would follow the will of God the second time God called on him to go to Ninevah and preach to the people. It is a fascinating story that's only 4 chapters long. I want to encourage you to read it sometime, and enjoy the story of Jonah. I will have to say, Jonah made the wrong choice when he found himself at the crossroads of his life the first time around. It is safe to say that he was the first to ride in a submarine, which was created by God.

Life will get complicated if we let it. This is especially true when we get our lives out of balance. We all heard it's a wise thing to eat a balanced meal and to have a balanced diet. The older I get, the more I benefit from watching my diet and eating more healthy meals. My choice of beverage is always water and I avoid soda products at all times. In the fall of 2011, I allowed my life and ministry to get totally out of balance. My problem was a lack of rest and a lack of prayer. What caused this problem is my passion that I have for the outdoors, God's great outdoors. I'm an avid deer hunter, and I enjoy eating venison, especially my own deer chili. On my days off, I am either on the water fishing or I'm in the woods hunting. I always have my Bible with me when I'm fishing or hunting. I guess I got a little carried away with the deer hunting. I would get up super early on my days off and be out in the woods very early before daybreak, trying to harvest a deer. This was a ritual for me that I soon would suffer for. I would try to fit my "quiet time" in with God while I was hunting in my ground blind. While in my ground blind, I would use my flashlight or wait until daylight to read a little while in my Bible and then pray for a short time. I was more dedicated to getting up early in the morning to go deer hunting than I was meeting with God and fellowshipping with my Lord and Savior.

As deer season progressed, I got bronchitis real bad. That stayed with me for over 2 months. But bronchitis would not keep me from deer hunting. I kept pushing myself anyway, like a fool, trying to harvest a big deer. One day, while I was hunting in one of my tree stands on a farm that I hunt in Waynesville, Ohio, I began to feel really weak. I had the chills and was coughing up a lot of junk. My day of hunting was over. With all the coughing I was doing I knew no deer would be coming my way. On my way home that day I stopped at an Urgent Care. After the doctor examined me, he informed me that I had pneumonia in my right lung. Man was I sick. I don't think I ever felt that bad in my life. I was extremely weak and even light-headed. I was sick for about 5 months, and it took another 3 months just to get my strength back. Who did I have to blame nobody but myself. I ran my body down by a life that was completely out of balance. I should have known better. Jesus should always have first place in our lives. Nothing or no one should ever take His place. Otherwise, that becomes like an idol in our hearts. It wasn't long before I realized what I had done to myself. I asked the Lord to forgive me and I vowed never to let that happen again. Nothing comes before my worship of my Savior. Jesus deserves the best of my life, the best of my time, my talents, my treasures, and my testimony. I suffered the consequences because I ran myself down, not only physically, but spiritually as well, all because I allowed my life to get out of balance.

A balance life is one where your heart is fixed on the Lord. This happens when you spend time sitting at the feet of the Master. You may ask yourself, how do you do that? Very simple, just determine to spend a quiet, uninterrupted time with the Lord and His Word. Make it a priority!

The classic example of this is found in the lives of two sisters, Mary and Martha. We find this story in Luke 10:38-42. Here we find only 5 verses that show the one thing that's the most important in our life. "Now it came to pass, as they (Jesus and the twelve disciples) went, that he entered into a certain village: and a certain woman named Martha received him into her house. And she had a sister called Mary, which also sat at Jesus' feet, and heard his word. But Martha was cumbered about much serving, and came to him, and said, Lord, dost thou not care that my sister hath left me to serve alone? Bid her therefore that she help me. And Jesus answered and said unto her, 'Martha, Martha, thou art careful and troubled about many things: But one thing is needful: and Mary hath chosen that good part, which shall not be taken away from her.'" Here is a great example of a life out of balance. Martha's life was clearly out of balance. Her sister, Mary, on the other hand, had a very balanced life. Martha was troubled with "much serving" and developed an attitude. I guess you could say she was a little mean-spirited and cranky. What a question to ask Jesus, if He cared. Then Martha tells Jesus what to do, get Mary to stop sitting at His feet and listening to His words. She wanted Jesus to tell Mary to come and help her. Jesus then sticks up for Mary, and lovingly rebukes Martha. Martha was very troubled and distracted by her "much serving."

What is it with you? What keeps you from spending time at the feet of Jesus, listening to His Word? For me, it was "much hunting" that caused my life to be out of balance. As a result, I suffered physically for it. Like Martha, something else was more important than being at the feet of Jesus. Martha made a choice, and so did Mary. To be sitting at the feet of Jesus, Mary will be looking up at Him. How awesome is that? Notice again what verse 42 says. "But one thing is needful: and Mary hath chosen that good part..." It simply comes down to making a choice. Life is nothing but choices, every day and every moment throughout our lives. So we need to determine to make that time, which I call a "time out" with Jesus, a priority in our life.

As Christians, we have that relationship as children of God, which never changes. But let me ask you a question. How is your fellowship with the Lord, your communication, your communion with Him? God wants that time with us at least every day, and if so, each night as well to spend time with Him. How many times do we try to fit Him into our busy lives and schedules when we have a convenient time? How many times instead of getting the best part of the day, the Lord gets what's left over at the end of the night? Our Lord deserves our best every day. Martha was troubled about fixing a meal for a crowd of about 16 people. She should've taken a break from working and spent time at the feet of Jesus like Mary did. Martha was a worker. Mary was a worshipper first, then a worker. Worship should always be the top priority of a child of God. Martha was troubled with "much serving" that kept her away and distracted her from the Lord. What is it in your life that does the same to you? Is it working too much? Is it gambling too much? Is it drinking too much? Is it fishing or hunting too much? Is it too much sports and entertainment? Is it much shopping and traveling? What keeps you from spending a daily quiet time at the feet of Jesus to hear his voice? For Martha, preparing a meal wasn't a sinful thing, but it was keeping her from spending much needed time with God. Maybe your life is out of balance just like Martha's was and just like mine was. Listen to what Jesus said in John 4:23. "But the hour cometh and now is when true worshippers shall worship the Father in spirit and in truth. For the Father seeketh such to worship him." Did you see that? Our Heavenly Father is seeking for us to worship Him. How do we do that? We do that by worshipping and honoring His only begotten Son, the Lord Jesus Christ.

I believe the best time to spend quiet time with God is in the morning. As you spend that quiet time with the Lord, listen for His still, small voice as you are reading your Bible. And always pray for His help before you read His Word. Psalm 5:3 "My voice shalt thou hear in the morning, O Lord; in the morning will I direct my prayer unto thee, and look up." That's our prayer and our worship to the Lord. Remember, Joshua 1:8 tells us to "meditate day and night" on God's Word, and to "observe to do according to all that is written therein..." The results will be a blessed life and a prosperous way. And according to God, you will also find "good success." There is a peace that comes in your heart when you are a committed follower of the Lord, but for Mary and Martha, there were some dark days ahead.

John 11:1-44 "Now a certain man was sick, named Lazarus, of Bethany, the town of Mary and her sister Martha. (It was that Mary which anointed the Lord with ointment, and wiped his feet with her hair, whose brother Lazarus was sick.) Therefore his sisters sent unto him, saying, Lord, behold, he whom thou lovest is sick. When Jesus heard that, he said, This sickness is not unto death, but for the glory of God, that the Son of God might be glorified thereby. Now Jesus loved Martha, and her sister, and Lazarus. When he had heard therefore that he was sick, he abode two days still in the same place where he was. Then after that saith he to his disciples, Let us go into Judaea again. His disciples say unto him, Master, the Jews of late sought to stone thee; and goest thou thither again? Jesus answered, Are there not twelve hours in the day? If any man walk in the day, he stumbleth not, because he seeth the light of this world. But if a man walk in the night, he stumbleth, because there is no light in him. These things said he: and after that he saith unto them, Our friend Lazarus sleepeth ; but I go , that I may awake him out of sleep. Then said his disciples, Lord, if he sleep, he shall do well. Howbeit Jesus spake of his death: but they thought that he had spoken of taking of rest in sleep. Then said Jesus unto them plainly, Lazarus is dead . And I am glad for your sakes that I was not there, to the intent ye may believe ; nevertheless let us go unto him. Then said Thomas, which is called Didymus, unto his fellowdisciples, Let us also go, that we may die with him. Then when Jesus came , he found that he had lain in the grave four days already. Now Bethany was nigh unto Jerusalem, about fifteen furlongs off: And many of the Jews came to Martha and Mary, to comfort them concerning their brother. Then Martha, as soon as she heard that Jesus was coming, went and met him: but Mary sat still in the house. Then said Martha unto Jesus, Lord, if thou hadst been here, my brother had not died . But I know , that even now, whatsoever thou wilt ask of God, God will give it thee. Jesus saith unto her, Thy brother shall rise again . Martha saith unto him, I know that he shall rise again in the resurrection at the last day. Jesus said unto her, I am the resurrection, and the life: he that believeth in me, though he were dead , yet shall he live : And whosoever liveth and believeth in me shall never die . Believest thou this? She saith unto him, Yea, Lord: I believe that thou art the Christ, the Son of God, which should come into the world. And when she had so said , she went her way , and called Mary her sister secretly, saying , The Master is come , and calleth for thee. As soon as she heard that, she arose quickly, and came unto him. Now Jesus was not yet come into the town, but was in that place where Martha met him. The Jews then which were with her in the house, and comforted her, when they saw Mary, that she rose up hastily and went out , followed her, saying , She goeth unto the grave to weep there. Then when Mary was come where Jesus was , and saw him, she fell down at his feet, saying unto him, Lord, if thou hadst been here, my brother had not died . When Jesus therefore saw her weeping , and the Jews also weeping which came with her, he groaned in the spirit, and was troubled , And said , Where have ye laid him? They said unto him, Lord, come and see . Jesus wept . Then said the Jews, Behold how he loved him! And some of them said , Could not this man, which opened the eyes of the blind, have caused that even this man should not have died ? Jesus therefore again groaning in himself cometh to the grave . It was a cave, and a stone lay upon it. Jesus said , Take ye away the stone. Martha, the sister of him that was dead , saith unto him, Lord, by this time he stinketh : for he hath been dead four days. Jesus saith unto her, Said I not unto thee, that, if thou wouldest believe , thou shouldest see the glory of God? Then they took away the stone from the place where the dead was laid . And Jesus lifted up his eyes, and said , Father, I thank thee that thou hast heard me. And I knew that thou hearest me always: but because of the people which stand by I said it, that they may believe that thou hast sent me. And when he thus had spoken , he cried with a loud voice, Lazarus, come forth. And he that was dead came forth , bound hand and foot with graveclothes: and his face was bound about with a napkin. Jesus saith unto them, Loose him, and let him go."

Here is one of the most incredible miracles of Jesus. We also have the shortest verse in the entire Bible, found in verse 35, "Jesus wept." We see Lazarus, the brother of Mary and Martha, was sick. Word came to Jesus from them that "he who thou lovest is sick." So we figure the Lord will respond right away to their need, but as you read, Jesus didn't respond right away. In fact, he purposefully stays away until Lazarus had died. And He even missed his funeral. I'm sure there was disappointment because Jesus didn't show up when they wanted Him to. But I'm here to tell you our Lord Jesus is always on time. He is never late, not like us. Finally, after Lazarus had been in the grave for four days, we see Jesus and the disciples show up. There was sorrow and grief, weeping and broken hearts when Jesus arrived. Seeing and feeling their pain, Jesus "groaned in his spirit, and was troubled" by the darkness that death had brought to these people. That's when he wept, when He felt their pain. Jesus now comes to the grave of Lazarus and tells them to move the stone that covered his grave. Martha questions the Lord, and tells Him that by now the grave sight wouldn't smell too good. Jesus needed the people to believe him and trust him even during this dark time. So they listened to him and took away the stone. Jesus prays to the Father, and after His prayer, Jesus "cried with a loud voice, 'Lazarus, come forth.'" When Lazarus appeared at the opening of the grave, Jesus tells them to "loose him and let him go." What a miracle, what a Savior, what a Mighty God we serve.

It wouldn't be long before the religious rulers of that day would plot to destroy Jesus. They were extremely envious of Him and His popularity with the people. They envied His following. In fact, they even thought that if they could get rid of

Lazarus it would be good because Lazarus was such a powerful testimony of the mighty works of Jesus. When Palm Sunday came and Jesus was riding into Jerusalem on a borrowed donkey, on Monday, "the chief priest and the scribes and the chief of the people sought to destroy him..." (Luke 19:47). Later that week, Jesus shares in the Passover supper meal with his disciples in the upper room, and He washes their feet. He institutes the Lord's Supper (Communion) with the disciples as well. Soon, Satan enters the heart of Judas to betray Jesus which he does for thirty pieces of silver, which was the price of a slave. In the Garden of Gethsemane, Jesus is then taken and brought to the house of the high priest. Peter denies Jesus three times, just like Jesus said He would. The men that were holding Jesus began to mock Him and to abuse Him. They even blindfolded Him and mocked Him as they were hitting Him.

Then Jesus was before the Sanhedrin, a group of about 70 religious elders and teachers who accused Jesus for blaspheme for admitting that He was the Son of God. Now comes the crossroads of Pontius Pilate, the man in charge of the government of Rome there in Judea. If there was ever a man that was at a crossroads in his life it was Pilate. In fact, he was stuck at his crossroads at least 3 times as he was face to face with the Son of God. The crowd accused Jesus of "perverting the nation" and other false charges. This group was upset because the people were honoring Him as king, and He was the King, and always will be the King of kings and Lord of lords. They could not believe that before them was the Christ, the Messiah. After Pilate talked with Jesus and examines Him, he desired to release Him. That was the right choice. That was the right way. That was the right direction. That was the right road to take at this crossroads of decision that Pilate found himself at. Not once, but 3 times Pilate says to this mob, "I find no fault in this man." Pilate was at a point of indecision, trying to avoid sentencing Jesus.

Luke 23:1-25 "And the whole multitude of them arose, and led him unto Pilate. And they began to accuse him, saying, We found this *fellow* perverting the nation, and forbidding to give tribute to Caesar, saying that he himself is Christ a King. And Pilate asked him, saying, Art thou the King of the Jews? And he answered him and said, Thou sayest *it*. Then said Pilate to the chief priests and *to* the people, I find no fault in this man. And they were the more fierce, saying, He stirreth up the people, teaching throughout all Jewry, beginning from Galilee to this place. When Pilate heard of Galilee, he asked whether the man were a Galilaean. And as soon as he knew that he belonged unto Herod's jurisdiction, he sent him to Herod, who himself also was at Jerusalem at that time. And when Herod saw Jesus, he was exceeding glad: for he was desirous to see him of a long *season*, because he had heard many things of him; and he hoped to have seen some miracle done by him. Then he questioned with him in many words; but he answered him nothing. And the chief priests and scribes stood and vehemently accused him. And Herod with his men of war set him at nought, and mocked *him*, and arrayed him in a gorgeous robe, and sent him again to Pilate. And the same day Pilate and Herod were made friends together: for before they were at enmity between themselves. And Pilate, when he had called together the chief priests and the rulers and the people, Said unto them, Ye have brought this man unto me, as one that perverteth the people: and, behold, I, having examined *him* before you, have found no fault in this man touching those things whereof ye accuse him: No, nor yet Herod: for I sent you to him; and, lo, nothing worthy of death is done unto him. I will therefore chastise him, and release *him*. (For of necessity he must release one unto them at the feast.) And they cried out all at once, saying, Away with this *man*, and release unto us Barabbas: (Who for a certain sedition made in the city, and for murder, was cast into prison.) Pilate therefore, willing to release Jesus, spake again to them. But they cried, saying, Crucify *him*, crucify him. And he said unto them the third time, Why, what evil hath he done? I have found no cause of death in him: I will therefore chastise him, and let *him* go. And they were instant with loud voices, requiring that he might be crucified. And the voices of them and of the chief priests prevailed. And Pilate gave sentence that it should be as they required. And he released unto them him that for sedition and murder was cast into prison, whom they had desired; but he delivered Jesus to their will."

Even Pilate's wife was trying to persuade him to let Jesus go and she referred to Jesus as a "just man." She claimed to suffer much because of a dream she had of Jesus (Matthew 27:19). Pilate would not listen. The Son of God stood before him. Pilate was now face to face with Jesus Christ, who was the Word of God made flesh. Pilate was hearing the voice of God speak to him but other voices would prevail on that day.

Luke 23:23-24 "And they were instant with loud voices, requiring that he might be crucified. And the voices of them and of the chief priests prevailed. And Pilate gave sentence that it should be as they required."

Even after Pilate had Jesus brutally whipped which tore his body apart he still had a chance to let Jesus go. Pilate was a crowd pleaser not a God pleaser. Pilate made a terrible mistake, a terrible choice when he was at the crossroads of his life with the Son of God standing before him. He wanted so much to release Jesus but he didn't. History records that Pilate's life was disgraceful after he allowed Jesus to be tortured and crucified. In just a few years Pilate ended up committing suicide just like Judas Iscariot did. Can you imagine when Pilate stood before Jesus on his judgment day? In fact, all of us one day will stand before the Lord.

Here's a question and it's very simple. On judgment day will the Lord Jesus Christ be your Savior, or will He be your judge? What He does with you will be determined by what you do with Him. Here's a question asked by Pilate in Matthew 27:22 "…What shall I do then with Jesus which is called Christ?" Now that's the question I ask of you at this time. At this critical point in your journey, you yourself are now face to face with the Son of God.

You are now at the crossroads of your life and the road you take will determine your eternal destiny. You must make a decision as you come face to face with the Son of God. You may say, "There's plenty of time for that, but not right now." Did you know, you are not promised tomorrow? Here is an interesting fact, according to the FBI crime clock: that someone is killed in an alcohol related accident about every 30 minutes. We have no idea when our time on earth is up. Some think there are many roads to heaven, or many ways to God. Jesus Christ claimed that He was "the way" to the Father. "Jesus saith unto him: I am the way, the truth, and the life, no man cometh unto the Father, but by me" (John 14:6). Now that was one powerful statement. Jesus claimed that He was the only way to God the Father. We are not talking about a religion here. We are talking about a relationship.

Here is a "comparison of World Religions and New Religious Movements" taken from the book *Changing Churches*, written by Dottie Parish. "Buddhism—Buddhists believe the purpose of life is to escape from the wheel of suffering through self-denial and detachment from the world. This usually takes more than one lifetime. Karma, or destiny, depends on behavior in this and in previous lives. Nirvana, or enlightenment, is attained by losing your individuality and merging with the non-personal spiritual forces. Buddhists don't believe in a god. Hinduism— Hindus believe in non-personal gods and goddesses, thousands of them. Hinduism says everyone is a god, and afterlife is a series of reincarnations dependent on their good behavior in each life, leading to become one and god. The material world is an illusion. Individuality is called Maya, which means, illusion. We are part of god. Islam—Muslims believe in one god, Allah, and Muhammad was his prophet. God is not a personal being. Muslims must recite the Qur'an over and over in the original Arabic, not violate many taboos, and do the will of Allah perfectly. Their faith is expressed in rituals. Judaism—Jews believe in one God, who is the Maker of all things. They believe the Messiah has not come yet. Conservative and orthodox Jews attempt to keep strict Sabbath laws, food laws, and holy days. Mormons and Jehovah Witnesses—they both deny the deity of Christ, believe in a new revelation, deny the sole authority of Scripture, and deny that salvation is by grace alone. Both are cults. Both are authoritarian, chauvinistic, dogmatic, legalistic, and intolerant of others. Scientology is a cult based on the writings of L. Ron Hubbard. Beliefs are a mishmash of Judeo-Christian monotheism, Hindu polytheism, and pantheism. Mankind is caught in a cycle of reincarnations. Pantheism—A belief that God and the material world are one and the same. God is present in everything. We are all part of a non-personal, spiritual essence."

Then there is the Unity religion, the Unitarian-Universalist, Wicca, Atheists, and agnostics as well. There are so many religions with so many different beliefs. And yet, Jesus Christ claimed to be the only way to God, and He also claimed to be the only way to get to Heaven. Christianity is all about a relationship with a personal God. It is believing by faith in the Lord Jesus Christ. His sacrificial death, burial, and His resurrection on Easter Sunday is the good news of Salvation. Being a Christian begins with the finished work of Christ on the cross and His resurrection. It is not about trying to work our way to have favor with God and doing good works. We can't be good enough to earn our way to Heaven. It's not about following rules, sacraments, or rituals. To obtain the gift of eternal life, one receives the gift of salvation only by the grace of God through His Son, the Lord Jesus Christ.

The religions of the world don't take care of man's greatest problem and the cause for the curse of death on every living soul, which is sin. That's where the heart of the Christian faith lies. Jesus Christ, God's only begotten Son, paid our sin-debt on the cross of Calvary over two-thousand years ago. The Bible states in II Corinthians 5:21 "For He hath made Him to be sin for us, who knew no sin; that we might be made the righteousness of God in Him." Because of the sin of Adam and Eve, (Genesis 3), sin has cursed every person with the death sentence. We are born with a sinful nature. Sin separates us from a holy God and eternal life in Heaven. Jesus said in John 8:24, "I said therefore unto you, that ye shall die in your sins: for if ye believe not that I am he, ye shall die in your sins." It's more than just knowing about Him, it's more than just a head knowledge about God or Jesus. It is so much more than trying to be a religious person, like the man named Nicodemus who came to Jesus one night. Nicodemus was a very religious man, a Pharisee who was a ruler of the Jews. He found himself at a crossroad in his life when he was face to face with Jesus Christ. Will he continue on his religious road, or does he take the straight and narrow way that leads to eternal life? Jesus tells Nicodemus that in order for him or anyone else to enter into the Kingdom of God, they must be born again.

John 3:1-21 "There was a man of the Pharisees, named Nicodemus, a ruler of the Jews: The same came to Jesus by night, and said unto him, Rabbi, we know that thou art a teacher come from God: for no man can do these miracles that thou doest, except God be with him. Jesus answered and said unto him, Verily, verily, I say unto thee, Except a man be born again, he cannot see the kingdom of God. Nicodemus saith unto him, How can a man be born when he is old? can he enter the second time into his mother's womb, and be born? Jesus answered, Verily, verily, I say unto thee, Except a man be born of water and of the Spirit, he cannot enter into the kingdom of God. That which is born of the flesh is flesh; and that which is born of the Spirit is spirit. Marvel not that I said unto thee, Ye must be born again. The wind bloweth where it listeth, and thou hearest the sound thereof, but canst not tell whence it cometh, and whither it goeth: so is every one that is born of the Spirit. Nicodemus answered and said unto him, How can these things be? Jesus answered and said unto him, Art thou a master of Israel, and knowest not these things? Verily, verily, I say unto thee, We speak that we do know, and testify that we have seen; and ye receive not our witness. If I have told you earthly things, and ye believe not, how shall ye believe, if I tell you of heavenly things? And no man hath ascended up to heaven, but he that came down from heaven, even the Son of man which is in heaven. And as Moses lifted up the serpent in the wilderness, even so must the Son of man be lifted up: That whosoever believeth in him should not perish, but have eternal life. For God so loved the world, that he gave his only begotten Son, that whosoever believeth in him should not perish, but have everlasting life. For God sent not his Son into the world to condemn the world; but that the world through him might be saved. He that believeth on him is not condemned: but he that believeth not is condemned already, because he hath not believed in the name of the only begotten Son of God. And this is the condemnation, that light is come into the world, and men loved darkness rather than light, because their deeds were evil. For every one that doeth evil hateth the light, neither cometh to the light, lest his deeds should be reproved. But he that doeth truth cometh to the light, that his deeds may be made manifest, that they are wrought in God."

This is referred to as a spiritual rebirth by the Holy Spirit. This occurs when one accepts Jesus Christ as their Lord and Savior. The heart of the gospel message given to Nicodemus by Jesus is found in John 3:16-18. It speaks of being condemned if one does not believe on Jesus. You may say, "condemned to where?" It will be a place of eternal separation from God, a place of eternal damnation, a place called "Hell," and the "lake of fire." That's why Jesus came, to take upon Himself the sins of the world when he was nailed to the cross. Jesus died in your place to offer you forgiveness of your sins. Romans 6:23 "For the wages of sin is death; but the gift of God is eternal life through Jesus Christ our Lord." Did you notice what that said? That eternal life in heaven is a gift only through a relationship with Jesus Christ.

When Jesus came to raise Lazarus from the grave, He told Martha in John 11:25-26 "Jesus said unto her, I am the resurrection and the life: He that believeth in me, though he were death, yet shall he live; and whosoever liveth and believeth in me shall never die. Believest thou this?" We can see that death is not the end, like some believe. Easter Sunday, the resurrection of Jesus Christ proves this fact. On the cross, Jesus paid the price for our sin. His blood and His life were given once and for all on that day. Forgiveness is now found by the love, grace, and mercy of God because of the cross of Christ. The empty grave is proof that death was defeated. On resurrection Sunday, we celebrate the glorious victory of our Savior over sin, death, the grave, hell, and the devil. The power of sin was broken. The penalty of sin was taken care of by Jesus, through the sacrificial death on the cross. But the presence of sin is still with us. Only by God's grace are we saved from the wrath of God to come. God is a holy God, a just God. God's grace is His unmerited favor to us that we do not deserve. His mercy towards us is that we don't receive what we do deserve. His justice is that His wrath will be upon all those who reject His Son, the Lord Jesus Christ, and sadly die in their sin, receiving what they do deserve, Hell. 2 Peter 3:9 "The Lord is not slack concerning his promise, as some men count slackness; but is longsuffering to usward, not willing that any should perish, but that all should come to repentance." This repentance is a change of mind that one turns his direction and his heart to God, agreeing with God about their sinful condition. Realizing that sin separates us from God, and all of us have sinned, we all need to repent of our sins. After admitting we are sinners, believing in the Lord Jesus is next. Believing that He is the Son of God who died for your sins, and was raised again the third day (Romans 10:9-10). This is the gospel. This is the good news.

God desires to draw all people to himself. It is up to us to choose to follow God's way of salvation through Jesus, or not. God gives to mankind the free will to accept His gift of salvation through His Son, or reject it. God will not force this decision on anyone. He desires that you come to Him just as you are and enjoy a right relationship with Him. This is what Jesus meant when He said to Nicodemus, "You must be born again." This also is referred to as being "saved." God has allowed me to share this good news of salvation, the gospel message to many people. I was so blessed to lead my mother and my father to the Lord, as well as my mother-in-law, Pierrette to the Lord. At my mother-in-law's graveside service, which I officiated, there were over 50 people who trusted in Jesus Christ as their Lord and Savior. It is a comfort to know that I will see them again in Heaven. I remember the day I baptized my dad at our first church in Franklin, Ohio, where I was the associate pastor. We were standing in the baptistery and I presented my dad to be baptized before the church. And as I baptized him, I said, "I now baptize you, my father, and my brother, in the name of the Father, and of the Son, and of the Holy Ghost. Amen." It was a great and glorious day that I will never forget.

The greatest day of my life was when I repented of my sins and called upon the Lord Jesus Christ to save me. And because I've made that decision, I can tell you that my life has been blessed. As I look back, I've made some bad decisions in my life, especially when I wasn't a Christian. It is a natural thing to be selfish and live for ourselves and not to follow God when you're not a Christian. It is a battle, even when you are a Christian, not to give in to the temptations of the old nature, your flesh. The apostle Paul describes in the book of Galatians this struggle between the flesh, our old sinful nature, and the Spirit. Praying everyday, studying the Word of God, and attending church faithfully will help you stay strong on your journey. Looking back, I can see how the Lord guided me with His Word and His Holy Spirit. As I look around, I realize I am right where God wants me to be, doing exactly what He wills for my life, being a servant of the Lord. There is a peace and a joy that come from being in the will of God. As I look around and see the blessings of God in my life, I realize it is God's reward to me because of my obedience to Him. Looking ahead, I'm just trying to trust Him day by day for the future. I know in my heart where God directs, He will protect, and where the

Lord guides, He will provide. Having a strong faith and trust in Him every day of my life is the key of staying strong.

I enjoy sitting at the feet of Jesus, looking up to hear His voice as I read His Word. But one day as Jesus spoke in Luke 21:27-28, "And then shall they see the Son of man coming in a cloud with power and great glory. When these things begin to come to pass, then look up, and lift up your heads; for your redemption draweth nigh." This is the promise of His coming after the description of the last days. We have seen our share of false teachers, false prophets and false messiahs. Many were led astray by the false predictions of the 2011 and 2012 by some false prophet's claming the end of the world. The Bible says that no man knows the day or the hour when Jesus will come again. I know one thing for sure, Jesus *is* coming again.

Here's my question to you: Are you ready to meet the Lord Jesus? Are you 100% sure if you died today by being struck by a drunk driver that Heaven would be your home? Statistics show that 11,000 people die every hour, 180 die every minute, and 3 people die every second. Steve Jobs' commencement speech at Stanford University included this statement, "No one wants to die. Even people who want to go to Heaven don't want to die to get there. And yet, death is the destination we all share. No one has ever escaped it." Philippians 2:10-11 "That at the name of Jesus, every knee should bow, of things in heaven, and things in earth, and things under the earth; And that every tongue should confess that Jesus Christ is Lord, to the glory of God the Father." Are you ready to repent and call on the Lord Jesus Christ to save you? Are you ready to receive Him into your life as your Savior? You now find yourself at the crossroads of your eternal life. You will spend eternity either in Heaven or in Hell, depending on what you decide to do with Jesus Christ. Jeremiah 21:8 "I set before you the way of life, and the way of death." If you are already a Christian, you may need to rededicate your life to the Lord, and surrender to do His will. Just pray and confess your sins to Him. Giving yourself fully to Jesus is so important. But if you are not a

Christian, and desire a right relationship with God, you can do that right now, right where you are. Go to a quiet place where you can be on your knees if you. Find a place where you will not be distracted. Bow your head and pray to the Lord. Turn to Him, confessing you are a sinner in need of His forgiveness. Acknowledge that you do believe that God's Son, the Lord Jesus Christ, suffered on the cross, shed His precious blood, and died for you, believing also in your heart that God raised Jesus Christ from the dead. Ask Him to come into your life. Tell Him that you desire to accept Him as your Lord and Savior. In the closing of your prayer to God, thank Him for saving your soul and blessing your life with the gift of salvation.

If you have done this, you now will be able to enjoy a walk with God on this journey we call life. The gift of salvation, this gift of eternal life you receive through Jesus is a gift you will never lose. His divine direction for your life is now available. Heaven's GPS will never need a satellite connection. You have been connected when you trusted Jesus Christ as your Lord and Savior. You are now on the straight and narrow way as you follow the Lord. The broad way of destruction which leads to everlasting destruction and hell is the road you turned off of when you turned to Jesus. One of our Lord's promises to you is found in John 10:27-30 "My sheep hear my voice, and I know them, and they follow me: And I give unto them eternal life; and they shall never perish, neither shall any man pluck them out of my hand. My Father, which gave them me, is greater than all; and no man is able to pluck them out of my Father's hand. I and my Father are one." You are now one of His sheep. In fact, the gospel of John is a great place to begin your quiet time with the Lord as you look up to God on your new journey.

Chapter Five

"LOOKING DOWN"

M y favorite Bible Verses are found in Colossians 3:15-17, with verse 17 being my life verse. "And let the peace of God rule in your hearts, to the which also ye are called in one body; and be ye thankful. Let the word of Christ dwell in you richly in all wisdom; teaching and admonishing one another in psalms and hymns and spiritual songs, singing with grace in your hearts to the Lord. And whatsoever ye do in word or deed, do all in the name of the Lord Jesus, giving thanks to God and the Father by him." While I was completing this book, I found a wonderful Scripture in my morning devotions that I have now added to my life verse. It is Psalm 86:12 "I will praise thee, O Lord my God, with all my heart: and I will glorify thy name for evermore." This is my desire, and it should be every Christian's desire each day. In fact, when you get a chance, turn to Psalm 86:11, and let that verse speak to your heart as well.

Another awesome moment with the Lord I experienced while working on this book just a few days ago was a direct answer to my prayer. I had been seeking the Lord's will concerning starting an archery ministry in our church called "Centershot": "Making Christ the Target of our Lives." This family outreach ministry will be a real blessing. It's sponsored by good companies like Mathews. As I was having my quiet time with God one early morning I happened to be reading in II Samuel 1 for my daily devotions. This year I am reading through the Bible again and I started with the book of Genesis. I usually read 1 to 3 chapters a day in my devotions. So this is where I happened to be on this glorious morning. And when I reached II Samuel 1:18, I was amazed as I looked down at the Word of God, which once again was directing my steps. God's Word could not have been any more specific this morning. Are you ready to check out how amazing the instruction of King David was in that passage, and how it related to my prayer request? 2 Samuel 1:18 "Also, he bade them teach the children of Judah the use of the bow..." Out of all the verses in the Holy Bible, which happen to be over 31,000 verses, how is it possible that I could be looking down at this one verse at this exact moment in time? As I said, I was praying about starting a "Center Shot" Archery ministry at our church. And I believe the Lord just guided my steps in the right direction in making this decision about this ministry. God is so awesome! He can and will do the same for you.

The cover of Time Magazine of the April 6, 1966 issue read: "Is God Dead?" What a dumb question? Then we have those who don't even believe there is a God or a Creator. They are called Atheists and Evolutionists. God calls them fools in Psalm 14:1-3 "The fool hath said in his heart, There is no God. They are corrupt, they have done abominable works, there is none that doeth good. The Lord looked down from heaven upon the children of men, to see if there were any that did understand, and seek God. They are all gone aside, they are all together become filthy: there is none that doeth good, no, not one." Genesis 1:1 says "In the beginning God created the heaven and the earth." That's good enough for me. God said it and I believe it, that's called faith.

Now think about how far our country has gone away from God and our founding fathers' desire to have God in the foundations of America. Just read the Mayflower Compact of 1620, the agreement between the settlers at New Plymouth. "In the name of God, Amen. We, whose names are underwritten, the Loyal Subjects of our dread Sovereign Lord King James, by the Grace of God, of Great Britain, France, and Ireland, King, Defender of the Faith, &c. Having undertaken for the Glory of God, and Advancement of the Christian Faith, and the Honour of our King and Country, a Voyage to plant the first Colony in the northern Parts of Virginia; Do by these Presents, solemnly and mutually, in the Presence of God and one another, covenant and combine ourselves together into a civil Body Politick, for our better Ordering and Preservation, and Furtherance of the Ends aforesaid: And by Virtue hereof do enact, constitute, and frame, such just and equal Laws, Ordinances, Acts, Constitutions, and Officers, from time to time, as shall be thought most meet and convenient for the general Good of the Colony; unto which we promise all due Submission and Obedience. In witness whereof we have hereunto subscribed our names at Cape-Cod the eleventh of November, in the Reign of our Sovereign Lord King James, of England, France, and Ireland, the eighteenth, and of Scotland the fifty-fourth, Anno Domini; 1620." I think this document is pretty clear on where we need to be!

I think about how the Declaration of Independence begins: "We hold these truths to be self-evident, that all men are created equal, that they are endowed by their Creator with certain, unalienable Rights, that among these are Life, Liberty, and the pursuit of Happiness." Did you get that part about "their Creator?"

America was founded as a Christian nation, according to these documents, which was evidence of the hearts and souls of our founding fathers. This voyage was "undertaken for the glory of God and the advancement of the Christian faith." God says in Psalm 33:12 "Blessed is that nation whose God is the Lord; and the people whom He hath chosen for His own inheritance." Psalm 144:15 "Happy is that people, that is an such a case, yea happy is that people, whose God is the Lord."

Let me recommend a great book for you to read: "The Harbinger" by Jonathan Cahn. It is "the ancient mystery that holds the secret of America's future." An incredible book!

While we are on the subject of books, let me share with you some others I recommend. "A Tale of Three Kings," a study in brokenness by Gene Edwards. I love this book.

E. M. Bounds has written several books on prayer, I recommend them all.

A.W.Tozer is a gifted writer, read anything that he has written and you will see why.

A book written by Candise Farmer, "Green Pastures of a Barren Land." This book can encourage people struggling with the disappointments of life, especially those who experience childlessness and infertility.

"I Never Thought I'd See the Day," by Dr. David Jeremiah. This book deals with "culture at the crossroads." This is a must read. Dr. David Jeremiah issues a prophetic warning: "We must understand that we are in a war for the very heart and soul of civilization or the consequences will be catastrophic."

Another great book is "Quiet Strength," by Tony Dungy. This book is about the principle, practices, and priorities of a winning life.

"Happy, Happy, Happy," by Phil Robertson of Duck Dynasty. What a great story of a life and family blessed by the Lord.

"Not a Fan," by Kyle Idleman. This book is about "becoming a completely committed follower of Jesus." In fact, on page 29 of "Not a Fan," Kyle writes about "a decision or a commitment," the story of Nicodemus found in John 3, which is the focus of the second chapter of his book. I love what Kyle says on the last paragraph on page 29, "So, Nicodemus finds himself at what would seem to be a surprising crossroads. He would have to choose between religion and a relationship with Jesus. There is no way for him to truly become a follower of Jesus without losing his religion. This wouldn't be the last time that religion would get in the way of someone following Jesus."

Amen to that, my brother! I was a fan at one time but now I am a dedicated follower of Jesus. I followed Him from New York to Jacksonville Florida and then He directed me to Ohio where He has blessed me with the privilege of being the senior pastor of the First Baptist Church of Germantown Ohio. I've been here for the past fourteen years as of the writing of this book. You want to see something amazing? This book was completed in the month of August of 2013. I told you August was a special month for me.

How about you? Are you Fan or follower? Are you just a religious person or are you a Christian? Are you one who has a personal relationship with the God of heaven and His Son Jesus Christ? It takes a lot more than just believing in God and trying to being a good person. It takes faith in the Son of God, Jesus Christ,our Blessed Hope.

That's what this final chapter is all about: to help you follow Jesus as you look down and ponder what direction your feet are taking. Where are you headed on the road of life? Where is your final destination going to be? Proverbs 4:26 "Ponder the path of thy feet, and let all thy ways be established." Think about where you are going with the decisions you are facing. Your ways can be established and are established by the One who created you for His glory and His honor. God has an awesome plan for your life. The Holy Bible is your roadmap for righteous living and a blessed life.

Here are some helpful scriptures from God's Holy Word to help you on your journey.

Joshua 1:8-9 "This book of the law shall not depart out of thy mouth; but thou shalt meditate therein day and night, that thou mayest observe to do according to all that is written therein: for then thou shalt make thy way prosperous, and then thou shalt have good success. Have not I commanded thee? Be strong and of a good courage; be not afraid, neither be thou dismayed: for the LORD thy God is with thee whithersoever thou goest." Remember this is the only place in the Bible where you find the word "success."

Psalm 16:7-11 "I will bless the Lord, who hath given me counsel: my reins also instruct me in the night seasons. I have set the Lord always before me: because he is at my right hand, I shall not be moved. Therefore my heart is glad, and my glory rejoiceth: my flesh also shall rest in hope. For thou wilt not leave my soul in hell; neither wilt thou suffer thine Holy One to see corruption. Thou wilt shew me the path of life: in thy presence is fulness of joy; at thy right hand there are pleasures for evermore."

Psalm 23:1-6 "The Lord is my shepherd; I shall not want. He maketh me to lie down in green pastures: he leadeth me beside the still waters. He restoreth my soul: he leadeth me in the paths of righteousness for his name's sake. Yea, though I walk through the valley of the shadow of death, I will fear no evil: for thou art with me; thy rod and thy staff they comfort me. Thou preparest a table before me in the presence of mine enemies: thou anointest my head with oil; my cup runneth over. Surely goodness and mercy shall follow me all the days of my life: and I will dwell in the house of the Lord for ever."

Psalm 25:4-5 "Shew me thy ways, O Lord; teach me thy paths. Lead me in thy truth, and teach me: for thou art the God of my salvation; on thee do I wait all the day."

Psalm 27:1 "The Lord is my light and my salvation; whom shall I fear? the Lord is the strength of my life; of whom shall I be afraid?"

Psalm 37:23-25 "The steps of a good man are ordered by the Lord: and he delighteth in his way. Though he fall, he shall not be utterly cast down: for the Lord upholdeth him with his hand. I have been young, and now am old; yet have I not seen the righteous forsaken, nor his seed begging bread."

Ps 40:1-8 "To the chief Musician, A Psalm of David. I waited patiently for the LORD; and he inclined unto me, and heard my cry. He brought me up also out of an horrible pit, out of the miry clay, and set my feet upon a rock, and established my goings. And he hath put a new song in my mouth, even praise unto our God: many shall see it, and fear, and shall trust in the LORD. Blessed is that man that maketh the LORD his trust, and respecteth not the proud, nor such as turn aside to lies. Many, O LORD my God, are thy wonderful works which thou hast done, and thy thoughts which are to us-ward: they cannot be reckoned up in order unto thee: if I would declare and speak of them, they are more than can be numbered. Sacrifice and offering thou didst not desire; mine ears hast thou opened: burnt offering and sin offering hast thou not required. Then said I, Lo, I come: in the volume of the book it is written of me, I delight to do thy will, O my God: yea, thy law is within my heart."

Psalm 119:105 "Thy word is a lamp unto my feet, and a light unto my path."

Psalm 119:133 "Order my steps in thy word: and let not any iniquity have dominion over me." "

Psalm 119:176 "I have gone astray like a lost sheep; seek thy servant; for I do not forget thy commandments."

Psalm 121 "I will lift up mine eyes unto the hills, from whence cometh my help. My help cometh from the LORD, which made heaven and earth. He will not suffer thy foot to be moved: he that keepeth thee will not slumber. Behold, he that keepeth Israel shall neither slumber nor sleep. The LORD is thy keeper: the LORD is thy shade upon thy right hand. The sun shall not smite thee by day, nor the moon by night. The LORD shall preserve thee from all evil: he shall preserve thy soul. The LORD shall preserve thy going out and thy coming in from this time forth, and even for evermore."

Proverbs 3:5-8 "Trust in the LORD with all thine heart; and lean not unto thine own understanding. In all thy ways acknowledge him, and he shall direct thy paths. Be not wise in thine own eyes: fear the LORD, and depart from evil. It shall be health to thy navel, and marrow to thy bones." This is one of my favorites!

Proverbs 4:26-27 " Ponder the path of thy feet, and let all thy ways be established. Turn not to the right hand nor to the left: remove thy foot from evil."

Proverbs 16:9 "A man's heart deviseth his way: but the LORD directeth his steps."

Isaiah 30:21 "And thine ears shall hear a word behind thee, saying, This is the way, walk ye in it, when ye turn to the right hand, and when ye turn to the left."

Isaiah 40:21-31 "Have ye not known? have ye not heard? hath it not been told you from the beginning? have ye not understood from the foundations of the earth? It is he that sitteth upon the circle of the earth, and the inhabitants thereof are as grasshoppers; that stretcheth out the heavens as a curtain, and spreadeth them out as a tent to dwell in: That bringeth the princes to nothing; he maketh the judges of the earth as vanity. Yea, they shall not be planted; yea, they shall not be sown: yea, their stock shall not take root in the earth: and he shall also blow upon them, and they shall wither, and the whirlwind shall take them away as stubble. To whom then will ye liken me, or shall I be equal? saith the Holy One. Lift up your eyes on high, and behold who hath created these things, that bringeth out their host by number: he calleth them all by names by the greatness of his might, for that he is strong in power; not one faileth. Why sayest thou, O Jacob, and speakest, O Israel, My way is hid from the LORD, and my judgment is passed over from my God? Hast thou not known? hast thou not heard, that the everlasting God, the LORD, the Creator of the ends of the earth, fainteth not, neither is weary? there is no searching of his understanding. He giveth power to the faint; and to them that have no might he increaseth strength. Even the youths shall faint and be weary, and the young men shall utterly fall: But they that wait upon the LORD shall renew their strength; they shall mount up with wings as eagles; they shall run, and not be weary; and they shall walk, and not faint."

Luke 9:23 "And he said to them all, If any man will come after me, let him deny himself, and take up his cross daily, and follow me."

John 3:16-18 "For God so loved the world, that he gave his only begotten Son, that whosoever believeth in him should not perish, but have everlasting life. For God sent not his Son into the world to condemn the world; but that the world through him might be saved. He that believeth on him is not condemned: but he that believeth not is condemned already, because he hath not believed in the name of the only begotten Son of God."

John 3:36 "He that believeth on the Son hath everlasting life: and he that believeth not the Son shall not see life; but the wrath of God abideth on him."

John 14:1-7 "Let not your heart be troubled: ye believe in God, believe also in me. In my Father's house are many mansions: if it were not so, I would have told you. I go to prepare a place for you. And if I go and prepare a place for you, I will come again, and receive you unto myself that where I am, there ye may be also. And whither I go ye know, and the way ye know. Thomas saith unto him, Lord, we know not whither thou goest; and how can we know the way? Jesus saith unto him, I am the way, the truth, and the life: no man cometh unto the Father, but by me. If ye had known me, ye should have known my Father also: and from henceforth ye know him, and have seen him."

Revelation 21:1-5 "And I saw a new heaven and a new earth: for the first heaven passed away; and there was no more sea. And I John saw the holy city, new Jerusalem, coming down from God out of heaven, prepared as a bride adorned for her husband. And I heard a great voice out of heaven saying: Behold, the tabernacle of God is with men, and he will dwell with them, and they shall be his people, and God himself shall be with them, and be their God. And God shall wipe away all tears from their eyes: and there shall be no more death, neither sorrow, nor crying, neither shall there be any more pain: for the former things are passed away. And he that sat upon the throne said, Behold, I make all things new. And he said unto me, Write: for these words are true and faithful."

As I look back, I thank God for His goodness and His grace. As I look around, I desire to serve God faithfully all of my days. As I look ahead, I will trust the Lord with all my heart. As I look up, I will praise the Lord and be ready for His return. And as

I look down on where my feet are headed, I will follow Jesus wherever He guides me.

Remember, where the Lord guides, He promises to provide. And where the Lord directs, He promises to protect. You have His Word on it! I will enjoy the peace of God as I obey His perfect will for my life, and so will you, if you follow Him and obey Him. The way you follow Him is by reading His Word and praying each and every day. His Book, the Holy Bible, is a book to be believed and a Book to be obeyed. You walk in His Ways by following His Word and by doing His Will each and everyday.

I praise the Lord for answering one of mine & Gayla's special prayer requests. All throughout the Bible you'll find the prayers of men and women alike. One of my favorites is the prayer of our Lord Jesus found in John 17. In fact that would be a great study and time of meditation, studying the prayers of the Bible. Most of the Psalms are songs and prayers. Another one of my favorite prayers of the Bible is found in Psalm 143. How I can identify with King David in that Psalm. And the prayer of David in Psalm 51, asking God to be merciful to him is powerful. I thank the Lord for all the prayers He has answered and especially for bringing Christian and Liliana into Gayla's and my life. What a blessing.

As we now approach the end of our journey, I hope you were blessed by this book. More importantly, my prayer is that you were blessed by trusting in the Lord Jesus Christ as your Savior. He will help you on your journey, if you let Him. He has made an awesome promise to you, that He will never leave you nor forsake you. I'm sure, like me, you might have thought at one time, that God had abandoned you. You might've thought that He was nowhere to be found. Let me assure you, God will never leave you if you are one of His children, never. We lose a lot of blessings in our life when we want to go our way and do our own thing. His peace, His protection and His provisions are some of His blessings in your life as you follow Him. God will seem distant at times, but if you search your heart you will realize that it wasn't the Lord who moved away from you it was you who moved away from Him and the path that He has for you. Remember, Jesus is only a prayer away and 1 John 1:9 says "If we confess our sins, he is faithful and just to forgive us our sins, and to cleanse us from all unrighteousness." What a loving Savior Jesus is.

If you have been blessed by this book please email me at: crossroadsoflife@juno.com

If you are ever in Ohio please come and worship with us at our church, First Baptist Church in Generation, Ohio.

I think there is no better way to end this fifth chapter than to share with you this beautiful poem by an unknown author. This poem has been such a blessing and help to me and to thousands of other people. Countless lives have been encouraged by these words. When you look down and trace the path of life that you are on, remember this heaven sent poem that I conclude this chapter with. It's a good chance you may need this poem one day when you find yourself at the crossroads of life.

"FOOTPRINTS IN THE SAND"

"One night I had a dream. I dreamed I was walking along the beach with the Lord. Across the sky flashed scenes from my life. For each scene, I noticed two sets of footprints in the sand. One belonged to me, and the other to the Lord.

When the last scene of my life had flashed before me, I looked back at the footprints in the sand. I noticed that many times along the path of my life there was only one set of footprints. I also noticed that it happened at the very lowest and saddest times of my life.

This troubled me, and I questioned the Lord about it: 'Lord, You said once I decided to follow You, You would walk with me all the way. But I have noticed that during the most troublesome times in my life, there was only one set of footprints. I don't understand why in times when I needed You the most, You should leave me.'

The Lord replied, 'My precious child, I love you, and I would never leave you during your times of trial and suffering. When you saw only one set of footprints, it was then that I carried you.'"

— several years later —

Chapter Six

"LOOKING WITHIN"

I t was Sunday, October 1, 2016, Gayla and I had been spending time in Virginia at our son Jason's to celebrate our grand-daughter, Evelyn's, 1st birthday, which was on September 28th. I was also scheduled to preach the next day, Sunday, October 2nd, at the Lael Baptist Church, which is directly across the way from Jason and Rachel's house there in Lignum, Virginia. It was about 5pm when Gayla asked me if I was planning on going deer hunting. As much as I have a passion for God's great outdoors, especially deer hunting, for whatever reason, the desire to hunt that afternoon left me. I have a great spot in the woods on my son's property, with some good deer on my game camera and some huge feral hogs as well. I was excited earlier in the week to hunt, but that changed once this day came. Gayla and I enjoyed spending time babysitting our granddaughter Evelyn while my son, Jason and his wife Rachel took the time to celebrate their wedding anniversary that day. They were planning a getaway for the night while Gayla and I stayed over to watch Evelyn.

It was about 6:15pm when Gayla went up to Evelyn's room to put some laundry away. I was enjoying some special time with my 1-year-old granddaughter, who was nicknamed "Peach." Around 6:30pm, Evelyn was starting to get fussy, and I thought this could be bedtime real soon. So I called up to Gayla that I needed her help downstairs to get Evelyn's bottle ready. After a few minutes, I came to the bottom of the stairs and yelled again for Gayla, but I heard no response. I went upstairs to Evelyn's room and found my wife on the floor, convulsing. I quickly called Jason and told him to call 9-1-1, and to please come home. I don't remember all the details, but Wayne and his wife Regina from Lael Baptist came to the house after I called them. Regina would watch my granddaughter until Jason and Rachel got home. Soon the ambulance arrived, and so did Jason and Rachel. Rachel stayed home to care for Evelyn, and Jason came with me as we followed the ambulance to the Mary Washington Hospital in Fredricksburg, Virginia. When we arrived there, the E.R. Doctor recommended that Gayla be transported to the V.C.U. Medical Center in Richmond, since she was having a stroke. So off we go, Jason and I, along with the ambulance to V.C.U. Medical Center. When we arrived there, the place was extremely busy with every kind of emergency you could imagine. They were even dealing with gunshot wounded patients out in the hallway, right next to our room there in the E.R. What seemed like an eternity, Gayla finally got a room around 3:30am. The reason she was transferred here was to correct a problem area causing the stroke.

Here we are, on Sunday morning, October 2, 2016 at the VCU Medical Center in Richmond, VA, and I'm wondering, "where are you, God?" As we were sitting in Gayla's room, my son Jason pulls a white and blue pen from the chair he was sitting in, and asked me if I needed it. Just before he asked me that, I was very troubled, because Gayla and I had no medical benefits, and just a few months earlier in April, we had switched over to Christian Healthcare Ministry. I was worried if I had made the wrong decision by switching to this "biblical solution to healthcare cost," but I can truly say that CHM has been a tremendous blessing to me and Gayla. Well, as I took this pen from Jason, I looked, and what was on this white and blue pen? "Christian Healthcare Ministry" and their phone number, and with that, my mind settled down and no longer did I have any doubts about CHM. I wondered if the Lord arranged that? I know my son didn't know what was going on in my heart, that I was worried about the medical benefits, but I know that God knew what was in my heart, for He was looking within my troubled soul from His glorious throne of grace. And with a simple white and blue pen, the God of Heaven brought a peace within my heart about the Christian Healthcare Ministries. What a mighty God we serve! He knows the needs of our hearts. In fact, He knows even our very thoughts.

I love these Bible verses that lets us know that the God of heaven is looking within our hearts and souls. Psalm 44:21 "Shall not God search this out? For he knoweth the secrets of the heart." Jeremiah 17:10 "I the Lord search the heart, I try the reins, even to give every man according to his ways, and according to the fruit of his doings." Luke 5:22 "But when Jesus perceived their thoughts, he answering said unto them, What reason ye in your hearts?" Matthew 12:25 "**And Jesus knew their thoughts**, and said unto them, Every kingdom divided against itself is brought to desolation; and every city or house divided against itself shall not stand." And some of my favorite verses are in Matthew 6:6-8 "But thou, when thou prayest, enter into thy closet, and when thou hast shut thy door, pray to thy Father which is in secret; and thy Father which seeth in secret shall reward thee openly. 7 But when ye pray, use not vain repetitions, as the heathen do: for they think that they shall be heard for their much speaking. 8 Be not ye therefore like unto them: **for your Father knoweth what things ye have need of, before ye ask him**." What an encouraging thought, amen! Oh, by the way, I think this is a good time and a good place to ask you, how's your prayer life been? Remember, spending time with Jesus is the "one thing that's needful" in all of our lives.

As Sunday afternoon came around, our son Sean and his wife Amanda, and our youngest son Justin arrived at V.C.U. Medical Center. They drove all night from Ohio to get here, after I called them Saturday evening. Later on Sunday, a few doctors came in to meet with me, and they showed me the scan of Gayla's affected area, which was the entire left side of the brain, which would severely affect the right side of her body—her right leg and her right arm. The doctors informed me this was an acute, major stroke. And since Gayla was on blood thinners they were unable to do a scalp-cut removal procedure to relieve the swelling of her brain. Now came the devastating news that overwhelmed my spirit: The doctors informed me that since Gayla's brain would swell, and they could not do this procedure, she would not survive within the next few days. One of the most heartbreaking decisions I ever had to make was to sign the DNR form. Just 2 weeks prior, Gayla and I had sat down at our dining room table to discuss our wishes in case of a situation like this one. We shared about what our wishes were for our funeral services. We recently had talked about this because I had just lost a high school buddy of mine, and he was only 62.

I cannot describe in words the overwhelming darkness that came into my soul. The despair was heavy on my heart. I could not even imagine what life would be like without my precious Gayla. As I shared this bad news with my family, I believe we were all in a state of shock and unbelief. For me, pastor of the First Baptist Church of Germantown, Ohio, the one who was always helping and ministering to so many needy people, now I needed the help. This question arose in my darkened heart: "where are you, God? Why is this happening to us?" The tears flowed, as I was not prepared for this deep dark valley of the shadow of death we were now in. I cried, "O Lord Jesus, how we need you now more than ever!"

Later that night, Sean and Amanda got a room in a nearby hotel. Jason, Justin, and myself were able to stay at The Doorways, the hospital hotel. The Doorways was such a blessing for the days I was there. Gayla's brother Dean, and her sister Karla would soon arrive the next day, on Monday, from New York. That night, Sunday, October 2 2016, I was begging God to touch my precious wife. I know that unseen, nail-scarred hand of my Lord Jesus can reach down from His throne of grace and touch my Gayla. I know my Lord Jesus is the Great Physician. Around 3:15AM on Monday, October 3, I was awake and soon on my knees by my bed, weeping and begging God for a miracle. I don't remember how long I was praying, but when I was done, I reached over for my Bible to read in the place I had marked the day before. I was now in the Old Testament book of Deuteronomy Chapter 31. I began to read by my cell phone flashlight, with my 2 sons still asleep. My eyes began to look down to verse 6, and there was a "peace that passeth all understanding" that flooded my soul. God's Word and His promise came to me in my darkest hour. He said, "Be strong and of a good courage, fear not, nor be afraid of them: for the Lord thy God, he it is that doth go with thee; he will not fail thee, nor forsake thee." Heaven came down, and glory filled my soul, as God once again gave me a specific word, His promise to my troubled heart. He gave me peace during this dark storm that was overwhelming me and my family. I believe and trust in His Word. I believe the Lord was telling me that Gayla would not die. I believe that somehow God had showed up and proved once again that He will never leave us or forsake us, just like He promised. Now I no longer had to question Him. I now no longer had that doubt in my mind. I no longer asked, "where are you God?" Now when I got to verse 8 in Deuteronomy 31, the Lord confirmed His promise again to me. "And the Lord, he it is that doth go before thee; he will be with thee, he will not fail thee, neither forsake thee: fear not, neither be dismayed." God met me on the dark crossroads of my life there at The Doorways of Richmond, Virginia that early morning. He was looking within to my troubled soul!

Chapter Seven

"LOOKING BEYOND"

———————— ∽∾∿ ————————

Monday morning, October 3rd, I couldn't wait to get to the hospital to share with my family what the Lord had given me, His promise concerning Gayla. As we all gathered together in her room, I shared with them all Deuteronomy 31:6 and 8. I told them I was not taking my Gayla back to Ohio in a box, but by God's grace, I'll be taking her home with me. We all circled around her, and with tear-filled eyes, we all called upon the Lord to touch her as we all laid hands on her. It was one of the sweetest prayers I have heard prayed by our family. My faith in His Word was moving me to be looking beyond our overwhelming thoughts of Gayla passing away here at the VCU Medical Center. My heart was fixed, and my spirit was looking beyond into a supernatural book, God's Holy Word, Heaven's G.P.S. I was focused on His precious promises, and now, by faith in His Word, I knew Gayla would survive and I would be taking her home with me.

When Tuesday, October 4th came around, the fact that the stroke affected not only her right arm and right leg, but it had also affected her ability to speak. This was extremely hard to accept, but I'm trusting in the Lord, our Great Physician, who touched my life again. Jason and Rachel soon came to visit, and they brought our granddaughter with them. Gayla's brother, Dean, had picked Evelyn up and brought her over to Gayla's bedside. With a radiant glow on her face, Gayla reached up with her left hand, gently caressing Evelyn's feet. That was precious to see. There was so much joy radiating from Gayla with her granddaughter there next to her. God is so good, all the time! Yes, grandchildren are truly a gift from God.

That day, our son Sean, his wife Amanda, and our son Justin had to leave and drive back to Ohio. Sean looked at peace before he left, and a few weeks later, had told me that he knew mom was going to be okay when she reached up to hold on to Evelyn's foot. That gave him so much reassurance and peace. Later that day, the doctors had come to meet with me. They said that they had never seen this before with this type of acute stroke, and that Gayla was very lucky that her brain had only swelled to 1mm. That was unheard of. I told them, with a great big smile on my face and joy in my soul, that my Gayla was not "lucky" but instead, blessed by God. She was touched by that nail-scarred, unseen hand of our Great Physician, our Lord and Savior Jesus Christ. It was time for these doctors to be looking beyond all of their known medical knowledge and reasoning, to the Lord of Heaven and earth. The doctors also told me that as she continues to improve, they were going to move her to a step-down unit, and probably on Monday, October 9th, move her to a rehabilitation unit for extensive therapy. I explained to them that we could not stay here in Virginia for an extended period of time. I needed to get back to Ohio. I told them that our church was back in Ohio, and we needed to get back home when it was possible. To my surprise, one of the doctors said that Gayla would probably be medically stable by Friday to be transported back to Ohio, but not by ambulance. The reason being, was that, Gayla would not survive such a long drive. It would not be good for her. They would only allow her to be transported by plane. Well, I said, "no problem." I figured our son Jason could drive my explorer back to Ohio. I'll get 2 one-way tickets and fly her back home. The doctors, with a smile, told me, that would not be possible. The only way they would release Gayla is by me hiring a medical transport plane with two pilots, two medical personnel, and with a special life-support stretcher unit. The doctors also informed me that it appeared that Gayla might have a mass on her right lung that might be cancer. Since we were heading back to Ohio, a biopsy would be done there at the Miami Valley Hospital in Dayton. I quickly refused to even allow that thought to consume me. There is no way. Not my Gayla! "Oh my," I was thinking, "how in the world can I make this happen—flying us back to Ohio?" I know now, by looking beyond to the promises of God. The Lord promises in Philippians 4:19 "to supply all your needs." Not our wants, but our needs. Gayla and I had a big need that I knew God would help us with. The first person I called was our daughter in law, Amanda, Sean's wife, who was working for Premier Health back in Ohio. The Lord put Amanda on my heart and I explained the great need that I had. It wasn't very long that she called me back, with the contact information for a medical transport company that was available. Praise the Lord!

So, I was told by the doctors at VCU that Gayla could be released and transported that Friday on October 7th under their conditions. I called the transport company, and they gave me two options to fly out: One was on Friday at 11am or 3pm. I chose 3pm, since Gayla's niece Vanessa was on her way to visit her from New York. The transport would be $13,800 or $13,400 if I paid it in full without using a credit card within 30 days. So I gave them my credit card information, and they gave me 30 days to pay it in full by cash or check. My God is able, amen?

Our church back home began praying the night Gayla was rushed to the hospital when she first suffered the stroke. Our associate pastor, brother Carl, was leading our church to do some serious praying on my wife's behalf. What a sweet spirit surrounded our church as they prayed night and day for my Gayla. My niece Amanda, my sister Mary's daughter in New York, began a "Go Fund Me" page for Gayla. She posted the last picture I took of her and our granddaughter while we were shopping at Walmart. It was time to be looking beyond my means and looking to our family and friends to help with this transport expense. To God be the glory, within 2 weeks time, over $15,000 was raised for Gayla. So many people gave to be a blessing. Especially our home church back in New York, Grace Baptist, where our pastor, Larry Holland encouraged the church to be a blessing to us. What a huge blessing they were! Pastor Scotty's church in Mississippi, Red Creek Baptist, was also a big blessing. And of course, our church family, First Baptist of Germantown, Ohio blessed us as well.

Friday afternoon had come, and the transport people were on their way. Amanda, my daughter in law arranged for Gayla to be admitted at the Miami Valley Hospital in Dayton, Ohio. Soon a team of doctors came into Gayla's room, after she was moved onto the special life-support portable unit. They were wishing us well, and this one lady doctor, with a tear in her eye, asked if she could hug me. I said I would be happy to. I could feel from her heart the love of God. I had signed all the necessary forms of release, and I was ready to fly my Gayla home to Ohio.

Soon, the transport team arrived, right on time. We were transported by special ambulance to the airport in Richmond, VA. There Gayla was carefully moved into the plane, and I took my place in the back. The medical personnel were sitting next to Gayla, to her left. And of course the 2 pilots were up front. It wasn't before long that we landed at Dayton International Airport in Ohio. Gayla was then moved into a special transport ambulance that took her to the Miami Valley Hospital. Soon we were in her hospital room, and my heart was just overwhelmed with praise and thanksgiving to God for Who He is and what He had done for us!

The weekend was filled with visits from our family and friends. One night a group of ladies from our church came to visit Gayla. As they were singing to her, she joined them! It was amazing to know that her stroke did not affect her ability to sing, only her ability to speak. It was so awesome to hear her sweet voice as she sang along with the ladies that night. I was so encouraged! But soon, that would change drastically.

Monday, October 10th came around with some bad news. The mass on Gayla's right lung, was indeed lung cancer, according to the biopsy results. Soon I would meet the cancer doctor to discuss possible treatments and surgery in the future, when she was strong enough. Right now, Gayla was too weak from the stroke to begin cancer treatments. I also met with her rehab doctor, that I'll call Doctor G. He was a blessing, and a godly man. He explained that Gayla would begin speech and physical therapy that afternoon and gave me her schedule. Her therapists were wonderful. I'm very impressed by each and every one who worked with her. I was focused on Gayla's recovery and praying I would be able to take her home soon. As each week went by, my precious Gayla was doing so well in all her therapy sessions and progressing rapidly. At this point, I think I was in a state of denial concerning her lung cancer. Deep down inside, I was trusting that God would handle it. After several weeks, Doctor G informed me that Gayla was ready to be released. He said she was doing amazing in her wheel chair, and walking with the aid of the physical therapist and with her cane. We would be scheduling more physical therapy sessions when we got settled at home. These sessions would be in our home.

Before we were set to go home, our son Jason had come to visit. He actually stayed with Gayla during some of her therapy sessions there at the Miami Valley. He had driven my explorer that I had left in Virginia back to Ohio. We flew him back when he needed to get home to his family in a few days. Her rehab doctor met with me the day Gayla was getting released, and shared with me this heartbreaking news: He told me that she was doing so well, but once Gayla started her cancer treatments, Chemotherapy, she would eventually lose a lot of what she had accomplished. That's not what I wanted to hear before we left for home. Thank God the doctor was honest as to what would lie ahead for us.

The day came for me to take my sweetheart home. I was so fired up! So happy. Before that day I had purchased a special bed that elevated and had a remote control unit. I was preparing the house the best I could for her arrival. I removed our door that leads to our master bathroom, to make it easier for her with her wheelchair. Everything was all set. Welcome home baloons were there at the dining room table, with flowers to welcome my Gayla home. Our family was waiting, and Gayla was all smiles when I wheeled her out into the hospital's parking garage and helped her into the van. Wow! What a feeling, what joy flooded my soul. There she was, sitting down beside me, holding my right hand with her left hand. As we were heading down I-75 south, getting closer to home, I began tearing up and praising God for His goodness. We finally made it home, and settled down to enjoy the special day. That night as we were settled to sleep in our bed, Gayla had nudged me because I guess I was snoring so loud that she couldn't sleep. She was very limited in her speech. Just one word she would say, and that was "yeah." I looked at her and asked her if I should let her sleep alone. She gave me a nod 'yes.' So off to the spare bedroom next door I went. The next day we went together to Walmart, and I put her in one of those handicap motorized carts. Boy, was that an experience! We laughed so hard as she was banging into stuff. I told her that she was always making fun of my New York driving. Now it was my turn to make fun of her driving. She looked so cute driving that cart.

The home therapy sessions were going well. The speech, physical, and occupational therapists were great. But soon, we were going to the Atrium Medical Center for therapy, since Gayla had met all her therapy goals at home. Praise the Lord! She was determined to get back to a healthy body. Her therapist would comment to me after we were there at the Atrium how great it was to work with her. What a testimony she had! She touched many lives in the Miami Valley Hospital, and now she's touching lives here at the Atrium. How blessed I am to have a godly wife like my Gayla.

Well, Christmas was now near and we would celebrate our Lord's birth at our home in Franklin, Ohio. Jason, Rachel, and Evelyn would come from their home in Virginia to celebrate with us and stay for a few days. When they did arrive, I no longer could sleep in the spare bedroom. Oh, by the way, I did purchase and setup a room monitor, so I could respond when Gayla would need me in the night. I would hear her call out "ok, ok." Those days with Evelyn being with Gayla were precious. Evelyn, I can see, was motivating Gayla, and putting such joy in her life. Gayla would love to hold her in her wheelchair, especially in the mornings when Evelyn would wake up. Jason and Rachel would bring her into our bedroom and Evelyn would lay next to her "Gigi" and drink her bottle of juice. Having them there was such a blessing those few days. Especially since I was back sleeping in my own bed with my Gayla. She loved it since I made sure I would read awhile and let her fall asleep first before I would call it a night. The day they left for home, there were tears shed and some sad goodbyes.

Now comes the day I was dreading. Driving to the hospital to meet with Gayla's oncologist to discuss her cancer treatments. This was scheduled after the holidays, when Gayla was strong enough to start chemo and radiation treatments. Chemo once a week, and radiation every day for a few weeks. We were told that Gayla had stage 2-3 non-small cell lung cancer in her right lung. We went to a meeting where we were informed of what to expect and what I needed to do as a caretaker. Thankfully, she would not be losing her hair. It would just thin out a little. My sons and I were prepared to shave our heads, in the event that Gayla would lose her hair. She was a trooper. And she had such a sweet spirit as we started her first chemo treatment and first week of radiation. After the 2nd week of radiation, the radiologist informed me that after she took a scan of Gayla's lung, the tumor was growing. Oh my! Why is this happening to her? God we need you! Please help us! The doctor said she would make some adjustments. The next day we happened to have an appointment with her cancer doctor. When he entered the room, he seemed very cheerful and asked how we were doing. I told him we were terrible. We're not doing well at all. He asked why, and I said to him, I guess you don't know that the tumor is growing, and that I think this treatment needs to be suspended? He apologized and said "I'll be right back." Soon, he returned and informed us he was starting Gayla on a new chemo treatment that would drastically fight this cancer, and he was stopping the radiation. He was right. After a few treatments, the doctor called me personally to let us know the scans showed the tumor was down to 50%. That was great news! But as she continued chemo treatments, she was getting weak. There were some nights when she would wake up sick to her stomach, and I would have to give her special medication. We no longer could use the regular toilet, but now the bedside potty. When she first came home from the hospital, one thing I dreaded to do was to cath her, so she could go to the bathroom. The nurses at Miami Valley showed me how to do it the day before we left. They supplied us with all that Gayla needed. That was rough but thank God I only had to do that about the first week that she was home. God gave me what I needed to be her caretaker. God never failed me. During these days, our sons Sean and Justin would come over to care for Gayla on Sunday mornings while I preached the 11am service only. One of the most cherished moments our church had was when I brought Gayla to church on a Sunday night in her wheelchair. What joy filled that place! One Wednesday night I brought her to church, and she was doing great! She walked in with her cane with me helping her by her side. You could see our church family over-whelmed with joy. The kids especially, who adored her, sur-rounded her and loved on her. There were many happy tears shed the few times that my Gayla was able to come to church. What an encouragement. What a faith-builder to our church family. God is good!

The news came after several more weeks of treatments that her scans showed that her tumor appeared to be nothing more than scar tissue. She was scheduled for one final scan, and then she would ring this bell and receive a certificate of completion of her cancer treatments. Praise God, now we can get on with our lives, and get more serious with her speech and physical therapy, so I thought!

It was a few months later, when Gayla was experiencing headaches. After setting up another scan appointment, I began to be very concerned about the days ahead. It was hard enough that she experience a massive stroke that caused her to have aphasia. The stroke also affected her right side, especially her right arm and right hand. The type of stroke she had was an ischemic stroke caused by a blood clot to the brain. The non-small cell lung cancer she was treated for, unfortunately was the type that could spread. And spread it did. First, the cancer showed up in her right side iliac. Then she had two tumors in her brain. She underwent laser gamma knife surgery that took care of the small tumor and shrunk the larger one to half of its size. So now that our insurance had changed to Care Source from Premier, we had to change doctors.

So 2017, into the early part of 2018, we saw some changes for us. We decided to sell our home in Franklin. I listed it for sale by owner on Zillow. Praise God, we got an offer in less than 3 days. We started looking now for a smaller, one-level ranch, with no basement. This would be so much better for Gayla, since our Franklin home was a two-level. After looking at a few homes, the Lord blessed us with a beautiful 3-bedroom, 2 bath, one-level, ranch home in the nearby town of Carlisle. I had some great friends of mine, Brian, Matt, Reuben and his family, build a beautiful back deck, with a ramp for Gayla. It was great to see the Lord's blessings during a very dark time in my life.

With our new doctor at Kettering, he was treating Gayla with Immunotherapy. This is a type of treatment that helps your immune system fight cancer. I was praying and hoping for a miracle. The thought of me losing my wife to cancer began to overwhelm me, especially at night while she slept. There was one Sunday morning, when I was in the shower getting ready for church, that Gayla had a small seizure. Then by the time I was dressed, she had another seizure, so I called 9-1-1 for help. The ambulance soon arrived to transport her to the hospital. She had a small seizure once before, when we were on our way to look at some homes with our dear friend Tina. But this seizure continued even when the EMT's arrived. After a few days in the hospital, she was released with some new medications. Each time she would spend the night in the hospital, I would stay the night with her in her room, right next to her on a cot. I wasn't going to leave my sweetheart.

So after a few months of Immunotherapy cancer treatments, and in-home therapy sessions, it was time for another scan to see how she was doing. This time, more devastating news. The cancer was flaring up in her right lung, and now it was spreading in her adrenal gland. The cancer doctor tried to comfort us by telling us not to worry, because her treatments would help. I was thinking, "help what? Help to prolong the inevitable?" Now I began to wonder again, "where are you, God? Why is this happening to my Gayla?" If there was a precious, godly, Proverbs 31 woman who deserved to be healed by our Great Physician, our Lord Jesus, it was my Gayla. I was trying to be strong, and not to be afraid like the Lord told me way back in the hospitality Doorway Inn in Virginia. God gave me Deuteronomy 31:6, but now the thought of losing her crushed me. What about our hopes and dreams? What about our plans to travel in ministry together? What about our plans to spend more time with our granddaughter Evelyn in Virginia? What about my life that depended so much on my precious wife by my side, my soul-mate? Why God? Where are you now?

Gayla ended up in the hospital again in July 2018. This time, some radiation would be scheduled, five days of it. I stayed with her again overnight. She had some pain in her neck now that they were trying to treat with radiation. I was praying so hard for a miracle. Praying for wisdom. I didn't want her to suffer anymore. One day the pain specialist doctor came in to talk with me. I know God sent her in at the right time. I was thinking about Hospice for pain management that morning. As this precious doctor shared her heart with me about Gayla's condition, I asked her about Hospice. Her face had this radiant peace about it, like an angel. She advised me that Hospice was Gayla's best choice now. She told me that Gayla doesn't need any more cancer treatments. She needed Hospice care now. I thank the Lord for His timing, and this doctor's honesty and compassion. So after 5 days of radiation treatments that was supposed to help with her neck pain, we were released and transported to Hospice of Butler and Warren County, across from Grace Baptist Church of Middletown.

The first week we enjoyed the staff, the meals, the room, and the care that Gayla received. The pain medication was working. She was feeling better and smiling more now. Her sister Karla came to visit from New York, and we had a good time eating Chinese food in the dining area. Now that the pain was getting under control, I was hoping to take her home, but Gayla soon got pneumonia in her right lung. The doctor informed me, that was not good and that she should stay there instead of going home. I had called our oldest son, Jason, in Virginia and told him I would fly him in for a few days, because things didn't look good for mom. That's what we'd call Gayla at times, "mom." Jason's visit was a blessing. One day, when all of our sons were there with Gayla, I stepped out to go home, get more clothes and check on the mail. While I was gone, our sons were cutting up with each other, and Gayla was getting a kick out of them together. In fact, she blurted out these words to them, "I want to say, brother time." At first they didn't understand, but soon realized that she was enjoying her sons spending time with each other and with her—precious brother time.

You know, while writing this, I had to take a few weeks off. Even now I am shedding tears over this precious memory. But I'm determined to finish this final Chapter with the Lord's help and blessing today. Soon Jason had to return home to his family in Virginia. The following week, Gayla began to sleep more. One of the precious ladies from our church, Norma, was now down the hall a few doors away. Norma was our ladies' Sunday School teacher, and one of the godliest ladies I've ever met besides my Gayla. She was a rock in our church. And now she's in Hospice getting ready to meet our Lord. I visited with her as often as I could, especially in the middle of the night I would check on her. Since I was staying with my wife in her room there at Hospice, oftentimes I would be ministering to hurting and grieving families at the loss of their loved ones. For a few weeks, I was surrounded by death and sorrow, trying to help those hurting. On Saturday, July 21st, at the age of 90, Norma stepped into glory. I was there as she passed. Her son came in my room with tears, asking me to come and pray with him in his mom's room. There she lay, absent from her body, but now present with her Lord Jesus in Heaven. I read a few verses and began to pray with her son, Clay Jr. and the Hospice nurse that was there also. Praying and weeping was what I was doing a lot of. My heart was heavy, and now I was wondering again, "Where are you, God?"

Our church had lost too many members in 2018—Steve, Maxine, Norma and our dear brother John Crowley who passed away in his sleep. What a blessing John was to our church. Gayla seemed to be sleeping now more than ever. Not even experiencing any pain now. Those who came to visit saw her sleeping peacefully with that beautiful face of hers filled with the peace of God. I was begging God, that He would please allow her to see and respond to our new grandson who was due to be born in early August and that He would allow me to be there when He would send His angels to carry her home. So on Friday, July 27th, our grandson, Torin Ricci was born. Jason and Rachel sent me a video, and I played it for Gayla when she was awake that late morning. She was so excited, and her face lit up with joy as she gave me a thumbs up with her left hand and said, "Yeah, ok! Yeah, ok!" She had a giant smile on her face. Late that afternoon while her nurses were changing her bed and checking on her, Gayla seemed to be staring at the ceiling. She seemed to be captivated by something that I could not see.

She couldn't tell me, but her eyes and her face were telling me, she might have been seeing the other side, with angels getting ready to come for her.

By Saturday morning, it seemed Gayla was in a deep sleep. By Sunday night, she never opened her eyes. Monday and Tuesday was the same now, with no response, sleeping peacefully. Although she was now sleeping, I would not leave her side at night. I would still sleep there next to her. Wednesday morning came, and by about 8am, her breathing changed. I called the nurse in, and she told me Gayla would probably pass sometime this day, August 1st. It was about 8:30 or around 8:40 when I was talking with Gayla, hoping she could hear me. I kissed her, told her I loved her, holding her left hand, and I said, "I'm not leaving here until you take your final breath." Just as I said that, Gayla raised up her head and opened her beautiful blue eyes. I was overwhelmed with the thought, just maybe I was seeing the miracle I had prayed for. Just maybe, I could take my sweetheart home. But as her breaths were getting fainter, I realized, I wasn't going to take her home. Jesus was. I looked deep, deeply into her eyes, and with tears in mine, I told her, "you're leaving me now, aren't you? Go ahead. This isn't goodbye. I'll see you again. Jesus is taking you home, isn't He?" And with that, my precious Gayla stepped into eternity, as the angels of Heaven came to carry her to meet her Lord and Savior, Jesus Christ at the gate of Heaven. I never cried so hard in my life. I was wailing in that Hospice room with a broken heart and an overwhelmed spirit. After awhile I called for the nurses, and they came to verify her passing. I asked if they could situate Gayla in her bed and make room for me to lie next to her. After awhile I went back in for about 20 minutes, lying next to my sweetheart, still loving on her with tears, holding her next to me one last time. I had to call our sons and her sister Paula in New York to let them know. Our son Sean and his wife Amanda were now on their way to join me. Before they would come, I stepped out to go to my car, and who meets me outside her room, my good friend, Pastor Brian Rose. He told me the Lord directed him to come now. As we embraced, I again wept bitterly in his arms. God sure knows how to direct people right on time to be His arms and hands to minister to people. I'm so thankful to God for using Brian that day, at that moment. Soon Sean and Amanda came when I was outside putting something in my car. They spent some time there, and Sean spent some time alone with his mom before we all left. Now we had to plan a funeral. Who in the world can I get to preach my Gayla's funeral? Surely I can't, there is no way I could, but God had other plans.

Gayla's celebration of life service was planned for Saturday August 11, at 11 o'clock at our church. The visitation was set for Friday, August 10th from 6-8pm. I was blessed, as was our family, to see the tremendous outpouring of the hundreds who came to honor her. Gayla had touched countless lives and had an incredible testimony of being a Spirit-filled woman of God. She was an amazing wife, mother, and grandmother. I was so surprised to see my older sister, Cecelia come with her husband Tom from Florida. Family from New York came from both sides. My younger sister, Mary and her daughter Amanda. My cousins, Mary and Angela. Pastor Reuben, and his family from Connecticut. My dear friend, Pastor Scotty Rayburn from Mississippi. So many other preachers and their wives came. So many whose lives Gayla had touched came. There were even some of her house-cleaning customers who came. The outpouring of love for my dear wife was so comforting to me.

You're probably wondering who would speak at her funeral service. Well, to my surprise, it was me. We were trying to see who we would get. Several of my dear pastor friends came to mind, but I had no peace about it. It was about a few weeks before Gayla ended up in Hospice that the Lord was directing me to His Word and His will for this day. Gayla was really tired that night, wiped out, so she went to bed early. As I went into the living room, I began to weep and pray, and the Lord was pressing on my heart this verse from Philippians 1:21 "For to me to live is Christ and to die is gain." The reality of my Gayla leaving me soon overwhelmed me that night. As I sat on our sectional sofa weeping and praying, I picked up my Bible. The Holy Spirit just kept pressing on my heart these words: "To die is gain." As I kept meditating on His Word, there was a peace that came to my heart. I picked up a small pad and pen and began to write as I felt the Lord leading me. I wrote down this acrostic from the word "gain." G – God's house, A – at home, I – in Heaven, N – no more pain, no more tears, no more death. As time drew near, I knew God gave me His message to share at my Gayla's celebration of life service. Besides, who loves her more than me, and who knows her better than me?

The message was: What did my Gayla gain when she died? (based on Philippians 1:21). It was a blessed day. I had a harpist play at the beginning and the end of her service. One of our teen girls, Chloe, played the violin special. My dear friend and gifted singing Evangelist, Dave Harney, led the singing, and also sang a special. We opened up with Gayla's favorite song, "Majesty," and I could sense the presence of God in our church. After the message, I extended an invitation for people to get saved. Praise the Lord, five people trusted the Lord Jesus Christ as their Savior!

I can say, being busy with so much to do right after Gayla passed away, kind of delayed the shock of the grief I would soon experience. It came to me like a flood, like a dark cloud. I was in a deep, dark valley, fighting off bouts of depression. I was never a depressed person, ever, but now my life was radically changed. My life seemed shattered, my heart broken, my spirit overwhelmed and contrite, as the Bible describes a crushed spirit. It was extremely hard to go to church now without her. Hard to preach without her there sitting in front of me in the third row, middle section of the pews. The fun we would have in church together before anyone else got there, I really enjoyed. I was extremely in love with this beautiful gift from God. I guess the Lord now thought it was time for her to be with Him. I really struggled for months, weeping morning, noon, and night. Pastoring and preaching were very difficult with my grieving, sorrow-filled heart. Oh, how I missed her! Our family and our sons missed her terribly. Her family back in New York, still shocked by her death months later. You know they say, "when you love much, you grieve much." Now *I* needed help badly. Life was getting lonely, and I felt so lost without her.

It wasn't long, then I started attending a Grief Share – Loss of Spouse outreach at another church. This was a tremendous help to me. In fact, after the first two meetings, God dealt with me. It was two things He directed me to do. One: wait on Him. Two: serve Him faithfully. I didn't feel like doing that, but I needed to trust Him and walk by faith, not by feelings or by my sight. Grief Share, along with my daily devotions began to bring some healing to my heart. God is amazing, He really is! So many timely devotions I read in a few months' time stressed Deuteronomy 31:6. On Christian radio one week, the featured verse they kept quoting was Deuteronomy 31:6. That was a week where I was having a *really* rough time, dealing with missing Gayla and fighting depression. God is always on time. One devotion was on Gayla's birthday, March 17. Oh how I needed this that day! It was from the Daily Bread devotional booklet. The heading was, "Standing With Courage," with today's reading from Deuteronomy 31:1-8. The last part of the devotion read: "Whatever darkness looms you, whatever terrors bombard you, God is with you. By God's mercy, may you face your fears with the knowledge that God will never leave you nor forsake you." Amen to that! A book written by my good friend, pastor/author Scott Miller. "Castaway" was a tremendous blessing to me along with his book on Angels. You can find them on Amazon.

So I guess we don't need to wonder where God is. So I can say, why even ask that question, 'where are you God?' But I'm sure some of you feel like that right now, or you have. One day you might walk into that deep dark valley of the shadow of death like I did, and wonder, "God where are you, and why?" The loss of a spouse is hard to handle. One of the emails I received from the Grief Share daily emails was titled, "One Flesh Relationship-Day 117." One of the books that was recommended that this email reflected was "Through A Season of Grief" by Bill Dunn and Kathy Leonard. This describes exactly how I was feeling. Here is what it read: "A part of you is gone. Your identity is shaken to the very core. You wonder if you will ever feel normal again, or if you will ever enjoy life again. When you lose a mate, you lose part of yourself, says Dr. Jim Conway. It's as if you've had an amputation of an arm or a leg. I think that you don't really recover. You adjust. And the process of adjusting varies with every individual. There's no formula. The pain that comes from the loss of the spouse is much deeper than most people realize, because in a marital relationship, two people become one flesh. 'The man said, this is now bone of my bones and flesh of my flesh. She shall be called woman, for she was taken out of man...' They would become one flesh (Genesis 2:23-24). When part of your flesh is abruptly taken away, there is a ripping and a tearing that leaves a huge, open wound. Until you've experienced the death of a spouse, there is no way you can tell someone how deep the hurt is. The Lord says that we are one flesh, and suddenly half of that flesh is torn from us, says Beth. 'Lord God, part of me is gone and will never be recovered. What do I do now? Amen.'"

I can highly recommend finding and attending a Grief Share—Loss of Spouse group. It will help you. I'm actually attending this 13-week session again a second time, which I find to be very helpful in my healing process. This was suggested to me by a friend in Sarasota, Florida that I nicknamed, "Sunshine."

So now what? I found myself at a major crossroads of my life. What do I do now? It's hard to pastor the church without my Gayla. It's hard to come home to an empty house, especially now that my cat Pepper has disappeared. At least she was some company and provided some snuggle time. But there was a void, and emptiness still, that only God can help with. So with much prayer and seeking God's will for my life, the Lord has directed me to resign my church and follow Him as a missionary evangelist. August 1, 2019 was also my 20-year anniversary as pastor, and Gayla's one-year anniversary in Heaven. A bitter-sweet date. August was always a special month for me, as I related earlier in this book. I'm honored to serve with my brother and president of ROMA, Walter Stevens. ROMA stands for Roma Outreach Missions Association. It is an outreach to the Gypsies of the world. I'm also an evangelist to churches. My ministry focus is, Exalting the Savior, Evangelizing the lost, Edifying the church, and Encouraging the pastors. I'm so blessed to be part of ROMA. I'm so excited to start my new journey. My dear brother Walter reached out to me a few weeks after my Gayla passed away. He knew what I was experiencing because he lost his precious wife Dolly after 45 years of marriage the year before. God knit our broken hearts together in a way only He can, and for His glory. If you'd like for me to share my ministry with you in your church, you can email me at TedRicci@romamission.com.

I can see how traveling will help with healing my broken heart. Not being home as much. Not being at the church without her won't be as painful. God is so good all the time. And I can't forget that I get to spend more time with my precious grandkids, Evelyn and Torin in Virginia. As I'm looking beyond to the days ahead, I don't know what the future holds, but I know who holds my future. My life is secured in His unseen, nail-scarred hands (John 10:27-30).

So as you continue on your journey and find yourself at a crossroads in your life, remember, God will help you if you let Him. Where God directs, He promises to protect. Where the Lord guides, He promises to provide. We will all face storms in our lives – physical, emotional, spiritual, and financial storms will come. There will be dark days of trials and tribulations, but in Jesus, you'll find peace as He promised. When I ended the first edition of this book, I ended Chapter 5 with the "Footprints in the Sand" poem that a close family member, Joanne, shared with me. As I share with you this edition, "Where Are You God," it seemed I was left alone, wondering oftentimes where God was. Maybe you know exactly what I felt. Here is a Scripture that brought me great comfort when my Gayla went home to be with the Lord. John 17:24 "Father, I will that they also, whom thou hast given me, be with me where I am; that they may behold my glory, which thou hast given me..." These words of our Lord Jesus, His prayer to our Heavenly Father made me realize, it was time for me to be looking beyond this life. My Gayla was now in Heaven beholding His glory. No more wheelchair, no more medications, and no more pain. She can talk now, walk, and enjoy the gift of eternal life that Jesus provided for her by giving His life for us on the cross (John 3:16). I know I will join her someday. How about you, my friend? Where will you spend eternity, heaven I hope?

I knew in my heart and believed the last part of Philippians 1:23 which states that, "...to be with Christ is far better." That, my friend, is looking beyond to eternity. Heaven or Hell are the only two final destinations after this life. Jesus is the only way to Heaven (John 14:1-6). When you have time, read these other Bible verses I shared in my Gayla's memorial service. Titus 2:5; Acts 7:54-60; Revelations 21:3-5.

I was thankful to preach for pastor Scotty to close out his preacher's conference in Mississippi in January of 2019. It really helped me to heal some, and I was blessed, especially being there with the McCormick family. In February of 2019, I spent some time in Florida with my dear brother Walter Stevens. I was blessed to attend the Bible Baptist Church in Bradenton, Florida and meet pastor Sal and his precious wife, Donna. I was very thankful to spend a few days with my sister Cecelia and her husband Tom. To close out my Florida trip, I was honored to preach at the Suncoast Baptist Church in Port Charlotte for my dear friend and former youth pastor, Pastor Eric McConnell. What a great day, and the Lord really blessed each service! Before I left to return to Ohio, I realized I was not ready for any kind of relationship, and dating was not a desire of mine, especially after watching Tim Tebow's movie, "Run the Race." That movie brought back so many memories of me and Gayla. I think God used it to tender my heart once more and to keep me close to Him.

In closing, I want to share some of His precious promises for you to meditate on. These verses are from Jesus and His Sermon on the Mount. Matthew 5:4 "Blessed are they that mourn: for they shall be comforted." Matthew 5:8 "Blessed are the pure in heart: for they shall see God." And as you find yourself at a crossroads in your life, remember His promises found in Deuteronomy 31:6 and 8, "Be strong and of a good courage, fear not, nor be afraid of them: for the Lord thy God, he it is that doth go with thee; he will not fail thee, nor forsake thee.... And the Lord, he it is that doth go before thee; he will be with thee, he will not fail thee, neither forsake thee: fear not, neither be dismayed." And remember that the Lord will direct you, if you let Him. So when you find yourself at the crossroads of life, you can look back, look around, look ahead, look up, look down, and remember God's looking within and sees what no one else can. 1 Samuel 16:7 "...for the Lord seeth not as man seeth; for man looketh on the outward appearance, but the Lord looketh on the heart." So don't forget to look beyond and trust Him. Proverbs 3:5-6 "Trust in the Lord with all thine heart; and lean not unto thine own understanding. In all thy ways acknowledge him, and he shall direct thy paths."

God bless you,
Ted Ricci
Colossians 3:17

CPSIA information can be obtained
at www.ICGtesting.com
Printed in the USA
FFHW021955171219
57080240-62665FF